HISTORY AND
THE CONTEMPORARY

ESSAYS IN NINETEENTH-CENTURY
LITERATURE

Howard Mumford Jones

MADISON, 1964

THE UNIVERSITY OF WISCONSIN PRESS

Preface

W E ARE, I believe, in danger of undervaluing or losing the imaginative support to be drawn from the past. That loss or weakening seems apparent both in American education and in American culture outside the schools. We insist upon dealing with the past in terms of the present tense and present problems. But our present problems will not be helped by assuming that past ages, past philosophies, and past works of art are distorted mirror-images of the contemporary. They exist in their own right, and they can help us in their own right. The seventeenth-century Puritans, the American statesmen of the eighteenth century, the greater personalities of the nineteenth century—consider what nourishment Emerson and Thoreau drew from Plutarch—granted history the right to exist as meaning for cultivated men, they did not demand that it be contemporary *Angst.*

To the statement of the general problem as I see it the first essay is devoted. Since I know more about the nineteenth century than I do about other great cultural epochs, this first essay is followed by two essays interpretative of that epoch, and these by a succession of specific interpretations of nineteenth-century authors, British and American, of importance in their own time and of importance to us until recently. These essays are endeavors to see what value their thought still has. Except in the case of Thoreau I have avoided the more fashionable names.

The origin of these essays and addresses is indicated on the first page of each. All have been revised for the present edition. My thanks are due to the editors of the periodicals concerned for permission to reprint.

HOWARD MUMFORD JONES

November, 1963

vi

Table of Contents

HISTORY AND THE CONTEMPORARY

History and the Contemporary

Prepared for delivery at Teachers College, Columbia University, and previously published in *Teachers College Record,* Vol. LXIV (May 1963), 625–636.

M Y SUBJECT is the relation of history and the contemporary, and I believe it bears not only upon the problem of culture in the general sense but in a particular way upon the problem of national education. I begin by noting the curious inconsistency between the national attitude towards history and the national inability to understand the meaning of history.

To the superficial observer no country is more conscious of history than these United States. The consciousness begins, so to speak, with the pious preservation of the Declaration of Independence and the Constitution under scientifically conditioned glass in the nation's capital. The federal government, the state governments, and many municipal, town and village governments likewise preserve historical structures, costumes, furniture, pictures, and so on with deliberate care. Historical museums are common, whether they are, like Williamsburg, Old Sturbridge, and Virginia City, outdoor relics or historical collections more conventionally housed, though equally valuable, like the Museum of the City of New York. Virtually every state requires those enrolled in school or college to be taught history, usually American history, and sometimes, as in Texas, the history of the state; and though much of this instruction is repetitious, and some of it resembles the history demanded by an unreconstructed rebel who yearned for an impartial account of the Civil War from the Confederate point of view, history is so widely studied that historical textbooks are a major branch of the textbook industry. I will not say they are a major branch of American literature.

Moreover, the nation views with pride the publication in innumerable volumes of the papers of such founding fathers as Jefferson, Franklin, Hamilton, Madison, and the Adamses. Among learned societies the American Antiquarian Society, founded in 1812, enjoys a respectable antiquity in our terms; most of the thirty-one organizations making up the American Council of Learned Societies operate within historical contexts, and the special distinction of the American Historical Association is that it was chartered by the Congress of the United States. No commonwealth but has its historical organization, and several have two or three. They all publish quarterlies or annual reports. There are innumerable local societies. The village of Peacham, Vermont, for example, has its own historical club, housed in its own building. In addition, there are other organizations for the pursuit of historical lore, from an association for the history of ideas to the New England Historical and Genealogical Society, and from the Daughters of the American Revolution to the Old Settlers Association of Montana. We do not have a Westminster Abbey, but what other nation has a Baseball Hall of Fame?

These examples of historical consciousness—I do not say they are equally impartial or scholarly—spring from a mystique: our sense of historical mission. From the assertion that God sifted a whole nation to found Massachusetts Bay to contemporary assumptions about the American way of life, this mystique persists; nor does the fact that communist countries, particularly Russia, have a similar sense of mission disturb us. Perhaps our most extraordinary triumph has been the imposition by the Old Americans upon millions of immigrants and their children of a standard pattern of historic myth, so that stories about Jamestown, the landing of the Pilgrims,

4

Washington and the cherry tree, and Honest Abe the Rail-splitter are a common core of legend to Yankees, Italians, Slavs, Jews, Orientals, and all the other racial groups that make up our cultural pluralism. Our good fortune is the greater when we consider the cultural tensions in other countries arising from the failure to achieve a common historical mythos.

Our achievement has inevitably advantages and defects. The great advantage I have hinted—the power for unification arising from our historical mythos, especially in moments of crisis. Even the governor of Mississippi, who passionately denounced the use of federal troops to put James Meredith into college, when the Cuban crisis was upon us, assured the president of the United States that Mississippi stood behind him. We have not split our continental nation into regions hostile to and suspicious of each other. We do not, like Great Britain, acclaim Robert Bruce at one end of the island and Oliver Cromwell at the other. We do not, like Canada, have to be perpetually tactful about two cultures. Even in the North Robert E. Lee is a great man, and the open display of the Confederate flag, which in a like case in another nation ought to be the signal for an uprising, is viewed by us as a pleasant anachronism, usually harmless. It yields even in Mississippi to the national anthem, and both North and South sing "The Star-Spangled Banner" or at least have it sung for them by an operatic soprano.

If all this be a boon, the defect of our conscious historicism is that, especially amid the siege psychology of the cold war, it makes for uncritical conservatism, an almost Byzantine rigidity of values. The flagrant abuse of the word "un-American" unfortunately testifies to the truth of Dr. Johnson's assertion that patriotism is the last refuge of a scoundrel. Some organizations dedicated to patriotism define historical values as values satisfactory to the organization dedicated to patriotism, and seek by pressure to impose their interpretation upon library and classroom, student and writer. Scholarship

5

vainly points out that the United States at its founding was a radical nation in a world of monarchies, a country viewed with distrust by all right-thinking Europeans, and that the republic was once a hotbed of social experiments, of which Brook Farm is the best known and the Mormon Church with its powerful economic organization the most durable. We have in this country no party of the left; and we have by well-meant legislation so cabined, cribbed, and confined critical interpretation in textbooks that they have, in the words of a deceased colleague, the air, if not of conspiracy, then of collusion.

But our emotional commitment to a righteous historical mission (was not the present age to turn into the American century?) clashes with another potent force so opposite to history that one wonders how the same culture can contain them both. The second power is the power of the contemporary. In other nations, of course, the hucksters of fashion persuade through advertising hundreds of thousands that not to be in vogue is to hang like rusty mail in monumental mockery. By mysterious processes difficult to assess, somebody somewhere somehow decides that sleeves must be full, not narrow —the waistline up, not down—the fashionable fall color rajah red, not the outmoded California carmine of last season. We talk seriously about built-in obsolescence. We put tailfins on our automobiles one season and remove them the next. We create the most admirable phonographs, electric typewriters, tape recorders and intercom systems, only to replace them next year by newer, more efficient, and shinier models. We demand the latest books, the newest magazines, the five-star finals, and replace one hit tune by another.

Our scientific achievement is immense, our technology one of the wonders of all time; but science and technology, business and industry, with all their blessings of health, comfort, efficiency, leisure, and happiness, also engender a contempt for the past. The past was all very well in its simple way, but we are well beyond it. Never was life so complex, frustration so universal, human affairs so tragic. The Greeks, the Romans, the Middle Ages, the Renaissance did not know how to think or to suffer. Newton yields to Einstein, Euclid to Gauss, Lobachevski, and Riemann, the cosmology of Humboldt to Gödel's theorem, Tennyson to T. S. Eliot, the notion of architecture as permanence to the notion of architecture as evanescence, *The Mill on the Floss* to Henry Miller. When knowledge thus fearfully expands and changes, when science undergoes these dizzying transformations, when taste revolves like a kaleidoscope, one is tempted to say with Faust,

> The ages of the past, my friend,
> Are to us as a book with seven seals.

If Spengler declared in *The Decline of the West* that the Faustian type is the epitome of modern man, he had in mind, I think, our impatience with tradition, our thirst for the novel and the contemporary, our impatience with yesterday and our eagerness for tomorrow. Do we not solemnly unveil the automobiles of 1963 in the autumn of 1962?

Our obsession with the present tense has profoundly affected education in the United States. The secondary schools and the colleges have experienced during the period of our existence as a nation at least three great educational changes. In its first phase, characteristic of American education from its beginnings to the Civil War, education appealed to two great absolutes—the Bible, which was patently the basis of a Christian nation, and the shining examples of Greece and Rome in their republican eras, which were manifestly models and guides to the young republic of the West. We were taught by Montesquieu, John Adams, James Wilson, and Thomas Jefferson, and by competitors for a prize offered by the American Philosophical Society at the end of the eighteenth century for essays demonstrating that the characteristic of a successful republic is virtue, that an instinctual *amor patriae* motivated the

7

best of Plutarch's men, and that education was to remind us of heroic virtue. Washington was depicted as the Cincinnatus of the West; John Adams, visited by the Marquis de Chastellux, was portrayed in the role of a Roman senator at Braintree, Massachusetts; and Jefferson at Monticello came out as a Virginian Horace, living philosophically on an American Sabine farm. Analysis of a long line of school readers culminating in the famous McGuffey series will reveal that fable, poem, and anecdote center upon the belief in Christianity and the belief in civic virtue. Amusing evidence of this classical absolutism can be found by scanning any American map, dotted as it is with names like Troy, Sparta, Athens, Syracuse, Rome, Utica, and Olympia, not to speak of such compounds and oddities as Philadelphia, Thermopolis, Eureka, Minneapolis, and Cincinnati. Bible names—Salem and Bethel are examples —are equally common.

In its beginning, the second great phase of our educational development overlapped the first. The second phase extended into the twentieth century and may be called the era of genetic or evolutionary explanation. The basis was historicism, a historicism that drew early nourishment from a providential reading of history. Providentialism was enriched by the acceptance of a romantic doctrine of historical nationalism from Europe and, by and by, through the rapid acceptance in all but fundamentalist areas of an evolutionary philosophy. On the one hand, ontogeny repeated phylogeny—so much so that in the early years of the Modern Language Association one enthusiast argued that the study of English in the high school should begin with the Anglo-Saxon tongue. On the other hand, romantic nationalism and the evolutionary philosophy combined to trace representative institutions upward to the Teutoburg forest and the customs of the freedom-loving Germans, and downward to the adoption in progressive western states of such democratic measures as the initiative, the referendum, and the recall. History was not only past politics, but politics sprang from past history. To understand anything meant to discover how it came into being. Literature was taught as an evolving process, and a history of literature was assumed as a matter of course to be the proper introduction of the pupil to the subject. Language became a problem in historical development, and if evolution did not apply quite as distinctly to the fine arts and music, musicology and the fine arts developed a biographical method and studied the evolution of forms. If classical physics and standard chemistry retained the absolutism of their eighteenth-century origins, geology and biology came rapidly forward. Meanwhile, educational theory was strongly colored by the Hegelian developmentalism of W. T. Harris and his contemporaries.

The third or contemporary phase of our educational development denies the premises of the first and second phases. One can see why this denial came to be. By 1910 the problem of the secondary schools, when they were absorbing thousands of the children of first-generation immigrants into institutions that had originally been established for middle-class Old American families, had radically altered from what it had been. The results were complex.

In the first place, the high-school curriculum, which had been shaped by representatives of both college and high school working together, came to be shaped by the high schools and by representatives of the schools of education, eager to prepare pupils for social and industrial living that grew more and more complex even while the pupils were being prepared. In the second place, well-intentioned child-labor laws kept in school segments of the adolescent population apparently uneducable under the old system and even, in the opinion of some despairing teachers, uneducable under the new. In the third place, the steady increase of our urban population and the decrease in our rural population rendered obsolescent, or seemed to do so, such familiar classics as Whittier's "The Barefoot Boy," Longfellow's *Evangeline,* and Bryant's "Thanatopsis," and simultaneously transformed Jefferson's dream of a happy agrarian republic into a dream of a lost world. In the fourth place, vast shifts in the labor situation included the increased employment of thousands of young women in office and factory jobs, and thrust upon both school and college demands for vocational training that swamped any central concept of culture and led, in the state universities in particular, to bestowing at every commencement a variety of bachelor's degrees incomprehensible to Thomas Jefferson. In the fifth place, the educational theory of W. T. Harris came to be replaced by the educational philosophy of John Dewey, who, understandably concerned by the failure of the standard curriculum to meet social needs, taught that democracy should begin in the grades or earlier and involve social living; and though the followers of Dewey caricatured his doctrine in applying it, the movement he inaugurated turned attention from the historical to the contemporary.

Finally are to be noted the disturbing effects of two world wars, the great depression of the thirties, the Korean campaign, and the cold war, upon one of the most complicated technological cultures in history. What good was Julius Caesar or a knowledge of French irregular verbs or comprehending the transcendental unity of apperception when the immediate problems before the young involved military service, a drive towards science, and the grimness of the post-Sputnik universe? The one thing needful seemed to many to be appropriate social and vocational training in the present tense for present problems.

Preoccupation with the present tense has not been confined to the public schools. It colors the values and assumptions of much scholarship. Scientists must of necessity live in present time and, in view of the enormous annual increment in scientific knowledge, can scarcely be expected to devote much professional energy to the history of scientific thought. The great interests of economists, sociologists, social workers, and social psychologists are necessarily in the fantastic world we have invented; and though anthropologists have never been more active than now, popular spokesmen for that branch of knowledge—Margaret Mead is an example—enthusiastically join in evaluating present problems in terms of what they know. Departments of philosophy honorably teach the canonical philosophers from Plato downward, but young thinkers find great interest and colder comfort in logical positivism, existentialism, and other modern relativistic theories. In departments of literature, aside from a few unshakable classics like Shakespeare, emphasis is upon the non-rational and the metaphorical—upon Kafka and Dostoevski rather than upon Jane Austen and Turgenev, who are too serene for our violent tastes. Even in history one notes the relative decline of the ancient world and of the Middle Ages, and the relative rise of courses devoted to more recent times and problems.

But perhaps the most singular instance of our passion for contemporaneity is found in the study of language, wherein a basic shift in emphasis has so altered both high school and college instruction as to draw a rebuke from James Bryant Conant. Having paid formal tribute to traditional grammar, structural linguists now assure teachers (or seem to) that spoken language is *the* language *par excellence* and that written English is by comparison a mere dialect. The resulting emphasis upon English "as she is spoke" is happily welcomed by persons who listen to the radio, the movies, and television, including educational television, wherein, in my experience, speaking is almost invariably sloppy by any standard of beauty, force, propriety, or correctness.

Not immediately relevant but amusing as an instance of the kind of English we have been accustomed to hear and read is George Orwell's translation of a passage of Ecclesiastes. The original runs thus:

I returned and saw under the sun, that the race is not to the swift, nor the battle to the strong, neither yet bread to the wise, nor yet riches to men of understanding, nor yet favor to men of skill, but time and chance happeneth to all.

Modern official English makes this read:

Objective consideration of contemporary phenomena compels the conclusion that success or failure in competitive activities exhibits no tendency to be commensurate with innate capacity, but that a considerable element of the unpredictable must invariably be taken into account.

I venture to put this into the vernacular as: "Buddy, it don't matter how cool you are, you can't always bet and win."

Parallel in another area is a remark by an administrative officer in a lesser Ohio college that, for mysterious reasons, insisted upon putting in a doctoral program. Asked how he could possibly administer such a program in the humanities in an institution with only a rudimentary library, he earnestly replied, "But you don't understand. The New Critics don't need a library. All they need is the text of a poem."

Although we have been plagued with the doctrine that every adolescent must be socially adjusted to achieve success—a theory that would rule out Henry James, Chekov, Napoleon, John D. Rockefeller, William Blake, most mathematical geniuses, Joan of Arc, and St. Francis of Assisi, to go no further—we are, conceivably, past the worst of the permissive period. What common sense and tradition could not achieve, fear of the Russians has driven us to. The most notable change is probably in science and mathematics, fields in which sleazy instruction and obsolete texts have led scientists to institute reforms backed by government funds in the interest of national defense. This movement has, rather oddly, carried along with it some tightening of standards of instruction in the modern foreign languages. More recently a committee of national importance has gone to work to establish direction and unity in the amorphous area of social studies.

Meanwhile the European lycée and the European gymnasium, comparatively unaffected by American practice, have clung to their traditional patterns of instruction in history, the languages, the classics, the arts, and the sciences. The young French student is aware of Pascal and Racine, the young German of Goethe, Schiller, and Kant, the young Italian of Dante and Manzoni as the young American is not always made aware of Franklin, Jefferson, Webster, Lincoln, Emerson, and William James. It would be difficult to prove that the younger generation in Europe is less well "adjusted" to life than is the younger generation in the United States, and possible to argue that the stability of educational patterns on a continent torn apart not long ago by World War II, the sense of belonging to a stable tradition, may be a power that curbs and stabilizes the restlessness of the young by reminding youth that the troubles of our proud and angry dust are from eternity, not from Hiroshima or Havana. I, too, am frightened by nuclear war, but a document rather more ancient than the reports of the Atomic Energy Commission has prepared me in some fashion to confront disaster:

Wherefore is light given to him that is in misery, and life unto the bitter in soul—Who long for death but it cometh not; and dig for it more than for his treasures.

. . . For the thing which I did fear is come upon me. And that which I was afraid of hath overtaken me.

The consolations of Job and the lamentations of Jeremiah at least remind us that the problem of social adjustment is somewhat older than the Declaration of Independence and the Constitution of the United States.

The inference is clear that I believe our present over-emphasis upon contemporary values in our schools and colleges, an emphasis underlined by worry and deepened by demand for scientific training, requires some sort of correction, that the source of this correction lies in history, and that if we are to maintain a balanced national life, we must fuse the needs of

13

technology and the needs of culture. I am the more persuaded of this truth for three further reasons.

The first arises not merely from the lack of any settled hostility towards the humanities among scientists but also from a positive thirst for richer and better knowledge of these branches of learning. Doubtless there are scientists who regard human learning, including history, as proper only to one's leisure time. Before one condemns this view, let him recall that for Schiller aesthetic activity was the highest expression of the instinct for play; and I read only recently an editorial in a scientific journal arguing that to the trained scientist the humanities offer no greater challenge than is offered by a novel. These vagaries are not, however, characteristic of thoughtful scientific men who, especially in the moral confusion created by the use of the atom bomb, deeply feel that humanity is more than the sum of its computing machines. Thus the Massachusetts Institute of Technology carries a vigorous program in the humanities through its four undergraduate years, and it is not unique in doing so.

In the second place, the successful application of technological devices to business and industry has created an embarrassing amount of leisure time, so much, indeed, that national gatherings like the Corning Conference and books sponsored by the Russell Sage Foundation have devoted themselves to the difficult question of its use. One of the ironies of history is that whereas to the generation of William Morris, when the work day was usually ten hours long, leisure loomed afar on the horizon like an earthly paradise, today, when labor is talking about the thirty-hour week, the disposal of the other 138 hours has become a national problem. We cannot spend all our waking time staring at television, going to spectator sports, or speeding over the country-side shut up in metal containers moving at seventy miles an hour past the billboards. The hucksters would, of course, like to monopolize our vacant hours, but a civilization mainly conditioned by advertising

14

arouses so little enthusiasm even among the advertisers that the novel of unhappiness on Madison Avenue has become a standard sub-species of American fiction.

The third reason rises out of our immense responsibility as guard and guide of the Western world, a position that alternately annoys and gratifies both our allies and our enemies. Our opponents, particularly Russia, have a special theory of history, certified by Karl Marx as the one true faith; our allies have each their own history, American ignorance of which gets us into continual hot water; and the so-called uncommitted nations, to our immense astonishment, develop interpretations of history that do not include the American century, at least in our terms. In a situation thus complex, it behooves us to move carefully; but it likewise appears that the apparent opposition between history and the contemporary weakens or disappears, and that history is one of the most powerful forces in modern times. What, then, is to be done?

The task before education is not easy. In the first place, the problem is not solved by merely requiring more courses in history. To add to the present mandatory instruction more courses in, say, the history of Asia or of Latin America or of Africa would merely clutter up a curriculum already crowded. The problem is not quantitative.

In the second place, even in the conventional course, one is brought up short by the quality of the textbooks now in use. From the point of view of literature there are, I suggest, three categories of style: good style, bad style, and textbooks. Few history books escape from the third category. I have read, or read in, a good many of them, and in my memory they fade with few exceptions into a common, an indistinguishable, gray. Scientific textbooks should, of course, be well written; if they are clear, we make no other major demand upon most of them. But history is a part of literature. The great historians from Herodotus to Henry Adams have been distinguished stylists, and the classics in the field are products not merely of accurate research but of imaginative vision, of profound commitment to humanity, of a keen sense of the tragic and the comic, of concern for the religious, philosophical, or moral meaning of human development. Our textbooks turn their backs upon these qualities. One does not expect all the members of the American Historical Association to write like Gibbon, Macaulay, Michelet, or Carl Becker, but is it not true that most of our textbooks in history are written not only by professors but also by the three gray fears—the fear of the young, the fear of pressure groups, and the fear of the teacher? These phantoms preside in all the offices of the textbook houses. The book must appeal to the young; the book must not offend the susceptibilities, moral or patriotic, of the John Birch Society, or the DAR, or the White Citizens Council, or somebody else; the book must not be beyond the comprehension of the teacher. One wonders in comparison how *Hamlet,* the vocabulary of which is difficult, the meaning of which is obscure, and the themes of which include both incest and an incitement to political assassination, ever gets itself taught in school or college.

The national culture would certainly be improved by better textbooks, but what would benefit us even more is a wider diffusion, a wiser understanding of the historical point of view. Doubtless the uses of history are caught between two platitudes, each of them simplistic: one, the doctrine that every age remakes the past in its own image, the other, the doctrine that the wisdom of our ancestors was greater than ours. As Professor Fritz Stern of Columbia has shown in a fascinating anthology, *The Varieties of History,* modern theorists of the subject from Voltaire to Toynbee have tried to establish— between the extremes, as it were—some governing philosophy of the historical process. These efforts are important, but perhaps too complicated for general influence.

Nevertheless, whether under the doctrine that we are the heirs of all the ages in the foremost files of time, or under the doctrine that the United States is the last, best hope of man, we may ponder the importance to education of two simple, yet powerful, truths. One is that the intellectual and aesthetic fashions of no age endure forever, so that there is no reason to suppose that the intellectual and aesthetic fashions now regnant in criticism and scholarship are any more absolute than those of the romantic movement or of the enlightenment or of the Middle Ages. The second is that the republic was created and shaped during its formative decades by certain philosophic generalizations that held true in their own time, and that, despite irrational psychology, may yet hold in some sense today.

What do I mean by these comments? Regarding the first one, I suggest it takes no great amount of reading in journals of scholarship and organs of criticism to discover that present fashion tends to divide all artists, but particularly writers, whether in past or present time, into the sheep and the goats. The sheep on the whole think well of man; the goats, with rarer wisdom, interpret him as a tragic blunder. An example from American letters will illustrate the point.

At the opening of the present century there was little doubt that Ralph Waldo Emerson was a leading American mind, and, unfortunately, very few persons paid any attention to a man named Herman Melville. At present, though it is not true that Emerson is in eclipse—his tough and resilient idealism can never be quite eclipsed—he is undoubtedly outshone by the more baleful star of the author of *Moby-Dick* and *Billy Budd,* who had, it seems, a tragic sense that Emerson had not. I have no desire to debate the question whether Emerson or Melville is the greater writer, for I do not conceive of literary studies as involving the award of prizes to First Boy, Second Boy, and Third Boy, and I cheerfully grant it was shameful to neglect so long the powerful and irregular genius of Melville. But when we concentrate, as in our schools we tend to concentrate, upon the sense of evil in Melville—or, for that

17

matter, in anybody else from Beowulf to Mr. Salinger—we not only forswear balance, but we give up history, which reminds us that there are other respectable ways of interpreting humanity. It is not only Sophocles who saw life steadily and saw it whole. The "Inferno" of Dante doubtless has its immediate, melodramatic appeal, but the *Divine Comedy* ends on a great C-major chord: *L'amore che move il sol e l'altre stelle*. It is not necessary to be a Catholic to understand that the human race is more than its frustrations. The same serene note appears in Goethe, who was no Christian, and in Marcus Aurelius, who was certainly a pagan. The primary duty of the humanist is not to follow fashion or to heap up historical lore, but is to consider fashion critically in the light of historical learning, and, achieving a responsible philosophy, to teach such wisdom as he can. I believe this duty falls equally upon those who teach in the public schools and those who teach in colleges and universities.

As for the great philosophical generalizations that lie at the base of our constitutional system, we live in an era susceptible to the Jeffersonian emotions but incapable of accepting the philosophy of Jefferson's age. We are emotionally committed to something called liberty, to a belief in the dignity of the individual, and to the right of oppressed people to be themselves, but we are bewildered when we attempt to justify our beliefs. We teach the triumph of rational inquiry in courses in physics and mathematics, and we teach a basic distrust of reason in much of our theology, our philosophy, and our art. It is apparently idle to point out that Sigmund Freud was a man of great historical culture whose thinking was strongly influenced by the Bible, by Goethe, and by Darwin, and that, far from seeking to destroy the rational basis of culture, he thought he was enriching and fortifying the long Western tradition. The enormous vogue of non-rationalistic theories of human nature is characteristic of literature in our time—in dramatic contrast to scientists confidently employing the tools of rationality and optimistically exploring outer space and distant planets, while the arts proclaim the fatuousness of mankind and the possible extinction of the race. Does not this curious opposition of values in our educational and artistic outlook represent the worship of one of those idols of the theater against which Bacon warned us long ago? "During periods of crisis," wrote Ortega y Gasset, "positions which are false or feigned are very common. Entire generations falsify themselves to themselves, that is to say, they wrap themselves up in artistic styles, in doctrines, in political movements which . . . fill the lack of genuine convictions." Surely, however, the historical meaning of democratic culture does not culminate in this wedding of opposites, this conjunction of a calculating machine and a psychoanalyst's couch!

I hold, therefore, that one of the overriding intellectual necessities in American education is the need for a richer, finer, more widely diffused and philosophical approach to democratic culture in historical terms. Even if this were not desirable in itself, it is forced upon us by our opponents, the Russians and the Chinese, who have a philosophy and a philosophic interpretation of the historical process. Merely to declare their philosophy wrong-headed gets us nowhere, either at home with our own people, or with our friends and allies, or with the so-called uncommitted nations. As a young Russian exchange student said in my house recently: "I came here to study history. The professors spend a lot of time attacking Marxism, in which I believe, but they do not seem to know how to put any philosophy in its place."

I do not say that there must be an official philosophy of history unanimously agreed on; I say only that a thoughtful consideration of the historic process that has brought the United States into being and long sustained it is basic to education in this republic. I do not think that doctrine should be established by the Congress of the United States or by patriotic groups or by school boards or by the American Historical

Association. I say only that we have too long neglected the truth latent in the great figure of speech with which Daniel Webster opened his "Second Reply to Hayne," when he said that after the marine had been long tossed about by the storm, he will be wise if he takes a new observation of the stars to determine what his course has been and whither he is bound.

The Peace Corps, traveling exhibitions of art screened by the State Department, productions of *Porgy and Bess* by American theatrical companies around the world, concerts of American music on the air, American news broadcasts over Radio Free Europe, the establishment of information centers in foreign capitals, the sending of Fulbright scholars and Fulbright lecturers to universities in foreign lands—these are very good things in their way, but they remain what they essentially are, instruments of propaganda—sometimes good, sometimes indifferent, sometimes, in their unexpected results, disastrous. They do not differ from the propaganda instruments of other nations. But a totality of statement, a totality of belief about the moral meaning of history and the relation of American culture to that interpretation—that is what I fail to find in our American educational patterns.

I repeat—and I cannot repeat too often—that I do not want either super-patriotism or super-propaganda. What I want is a refusal to interpret the story of man in terms of contemporary anxiety only, and a belief that during the centuries that look down upon us from the Pyramids, in Napoleon's phrase, human life has struggled forward to dignity and value. To master this kind of interpretation takes, I grant, a maturity we have not achieved in our schools and in our universities. But if, in Archibald MacLeish's words, America was promises, our allies, our enemies, and our hesitant and neutral neighbors have some right to know and an inevitable interest in learning how the promissory notes were paid and in what coinage.

That the United States shall understand itself in philosophical terms mediating between the eighteenth-century values into which it was born and a twentieth-century denial of many of these values—this is a demanding task. To ask that the Americans, or a significant fraction of them holding key positions in education, industry, and government, shall likewise try to comprehend the development and sensitivities of the rest of the world—this, indeed, looks like an impossible assignment. I admit the difficulty, but I insist upon the necessity of the burden, which scholarship has nobly begun to bear. To translate this knowledge as we gain it into some sort of viable philosophy is, along with our support of science, the great educational problem of our day. It can be done only through enlightened scholarship. I, for one, have grown weary of historical relativism cynically misread. I hold that the imperative task of scholarship is not, God knows, to be didactic and commonplace, but rather to lead young men and women, boys and girls, to understand that history is something they cannot escape and so to inform and infect other parts of their education with this knowledge that they come to understand that a responsible culture is more than vocationalism, social adjustment, getting your lessons, and a general sense of frustration. Macaulay's great picture of the New Zealander standing on the ruins of London Bridge and contemplating the lost glories of the British Empire has great fascination, but I should like to juxtapose a passage from a document we helped to frame in 1944 and 1945:

Determined to save succeeding generations from the scourge of war, which twice in our lifetime has brought untold sorrow to mankind, and

To reaffirm faith in fundamental human rights, in the dignity and worth of the human person, in the equal rights of men and women, and of nations large and small, and

To establish conditions under which justice and a respect for the obligations arising from treaties and other sources of international law can be maintained, and

To promote social progress and better standards of life in larger freedom, and for these ends

21

To practice tolerance and live together in peace with one another as good neighbors, and

To unite our strength to maintain international peace and security, and

To secure, by the acceptance of principles and the institution of methods, that armed force shall not be used, save in the common interest, and

To employ international machinery for the promotion of the economic and social advancement of all peoples,

the signatories "resolve to combine our efforts to accomplish these aims."

Such is the opening of the Charter of the United Nations. The statement concerns the ultimate purpose of the historical process interpreted for humane and humanitarian ends. If this be not the purpose and meaning of history, why do we study it at all?

The Greatness
of the Nineteenth Century

Previously published in *Harvard Library Bulletin,* Vol. XI (Winter 1957), 5–20.

Scholarship is accustomed to great, evasive terms in cultural history, such as the Renaissance, the Middle Ages, the Hellenistic world; and if occasional attempts are made to overthrow or shrink these concepts (efforts to define the Renaissance seem to want to abolish it), the giant phrases continue to hold their meaning and their excitement. Even smaller arcs of time may glow with the same intellectual zest. One can, for example, be a Miltonic expert, a student of the Enlightenment, or a specialist in the times of Chaucer. Enthusiasm of this kind creates those useful institutions, the Classical Association, the Chaucer Society, and the Mediaeval Academy of America.

Has not the time arrived to admit the Nineteenth Century into the circle of these rich, imaginative words? Not the Victorian Age only, not the Genteel Tradition, not the triumph of the Bourgeoisie, not the Age of Imperialism alone, but the whole of the Nineteenth Century as a sweeping cultural term? The Age of Steam is almost as remote, in one sense, as the Age of Sail, and we ought to put it into order. Over half a hundred years have elapsed since Victoria peacefully died, and virtually half a century has gone since Nicholas II was put to death; surely we can begin to see a great age in proper perspective and to salvage what we can of it before every-

23

thing goes. Salvaging cannot be too soon begun. Bombing destroyed much; and in the United States nineteenth-century domestic architecture disappears along the old-fashioned avenues of emptied homes in Chicago or Cleveland, Rochester or Detroit, where chain-stores, funeral homes, business colleges, and second-hand-car lots crowd towards the curb, their neon lights blinding us to the few mansard roofs behind them. Photographers who turn their cameras incessantly upon structures from the Greek revival do not interest themselves in these stately dwellings except as examples of bad taste.

This, however, is to digress from the central truth that the nineteenth century is one of the most brilliant cultural epochs in all history, whether you measure it by genius or by change. It belongs with the thirteenth, which some enthusiast once dubbed the greatest of centuries. It surpasses the Age of Enlightenment in the width of its many interests, the combination of theory and application it gives us. It has the scope and significance of the Age of Pericles, for surely the century of Beethoven, Goethe, Riemann, Darwin, Eads, Marx, Goya, Turner, Helmholtz, Lincoln, Hegel, and Pasteur does not have to pale its intellectual fires before even the Greeks, to the study of whom it devoted brilliant scholarship and critical acumen.

If the greatness of the nineteenth century as an autonomous cultural unit has not been more commonly acclaimed, it is at least possible to see why. Obviously until now we have been too close to this magnificent time to see it as it was. The antimacassars and the Biedermeier furniture have got in the way; the Albert Memorial and the operas of Meyerbeer are too loud, each in its own fashion. But time diminishes this disproportion, and we can now bestir ourselves to take juster measurements.

Latterly intellectual fashion has been all for the seventeenth century, and this for at least two understandable reasons.

24

One arises from the truth that a great many components of modernity—for example, the rudiments of modern science—appear in that age. Logically the study of origins should lead to curiosity about their results and so bring us straight to Huxley's laboratory and Agassiz's glaciers; but we leap over these things as too obvious, and worry about discontinuity and an expanding universe. The great work of the nineteenth-century men is taken for granted; an instance is the Mendelian theory. And a second reason for our disproportionate sympathy for the seventeenth-century mean is that we feel they would understand our *Weltschmerz,* could they but know it, whereas the contemporaries of Victor Hugo or Manzoni could not. To make this come out we have to proclaim Kierkegaard and forget Schopenhauer, believe that Nietzsche was a wise man and Tennyson a foolish one, and prefer Böcklin's "Toteninsel" to Seurat's "Ile de la Grande Jatte," and some of these things we do in a halfhearted way, and some we cannot bring ourselves to do. The despair of Pascal was a great and real despair, but who shall say whether it was greater than the despair of Leopardi or of Thomas Hardy? I do not know how to measure truth by amounts of misery, but let us not forget that the most philosophic emperor of that happiest of times, the Age of the Antonines, was of so melancholy a cast that all he could say of life in his *Meditations* was: "You have made the voyage. Now get out."

A third difficulty, unconnected with either symbolism or the seventeenth century, is to know precisely when the nineteenth century ended and when it began. We have never agreed as to the end of a century, but if we content ourselves with calendar time, in terms of American history it is at least interesting to note that in 1800–1801 Jefferson and Burr defeated the Federalists, whom we somehow persistently associate with wigs and knee breeches, and that this defeat marks the emergence of a popular, even a populist, faction, and the end of the dignified eighteenth-century world organized into rank and class. Dignity went out; democracy came in. At the other end of the arc McKinley and Roosevelt beat Bryan and Adlai Stevenson, and upon the death of McKinley at the hands of a nineteenth-century assassin in 1901, Roosevelt and the twentieth century captured the White House. The doctrine of Montesquieu about the balance of powers faded before the ebullience of the Big Stick, publicity became an organ of government, and Herbert Croly's *The Promise of American Life* turned into the gospel of a new dispensation.

This, however, is to see the nineteenth century in terms of an American parochialism, and I, for one, would prefer to read the century as stretching from violence to violence—from the French Revolution of 1789 to the Russian Revolution of 1917. In the one case, that last relic of the Middle Ages, the divine right of kings, left Western Europe forever; in the other, the divine right of kings departed from Eastern Europe, and thereafter the scanty Occidental prong of the greatest land mass in the world was to live its life more and more under the shadow of Asia, as Western Europe declined and Communist Russia increased in power and urgency from 1917 to the present. Neither the Marshall Plan nor the North Atlantic Treaty Organization could restore the splendid empires of the French, the Dutch, the Germans, the Spanish, and the British after 1945. Nineteenth-century imperialism became one with Nineveh and Tyre.

Whether one chooses the one set of brackets or the other, what an extraordinary set of inventions, discoveries, applications, and theories present themselves! The steam engine, the railway, the steamship, the submarine, the streetcar, the subway, the automobile are creations of the nineteenth century. So are the motion picture and wireless; so, too, is photography; so are the skyscraper, the mechanical reaper, the modern steel mill, the modern textile factory; electric power and the electric light (and of course the cable car); the

26

use of gas for illuminating purposes; the rotary press, the steel engraving, and the electroplate; the breech-loading rifle and a variety of other instruments of destruction, including the Gatling gun and the torpedo; the modern rocket; the coupon bond; postage stamps; the cheap newspaper and the cheap magazine; the public library; education at the cost of the state; and heaven knows what advances in medicine and surgery, including, of course, the principle of asepsis and the discovery of anaesthesia. Darwinian evolution and the Mendelian doctrine of the genes; the germ theory; the X ray; non-Euclidean geometry; the statement of the principles of thermodynamics; most of modern chemistry. The mind grows dizzy before this brilliant procession, as more and more novelties—the typewriter, the fountain pen, the Dewey decimal system, modern telescopes, modern microscopes—crowd into view. I omit a vast number of merely technological advances. One apologizes for so elementary a device as this casual listing, found in any historical textbook, but as so often happens, the elementary things sometimes get overlooked. No century in the history of mankind is more charged with restless intellectual energy.

This same gigantic energy conditions the bad taste of the nineteenth century—that is, of the Victorian world, the Second Empire, and the generation of General Grant. We who demand plain surfaces are appalled at the scrollwork, the jigsaw festoons, the carpenter's frenzy, the anarchy of lines that lead nowhere, of whorls that enclose nothing except smaller whorls, the imitativeness that turns iron into wood, tin into silver, brass into ormolu, and confounds all the properties of materials by pretending that everything is something else. Who that has looked at a catalog of the Crystal Palace or at pictures of the buildings at the Philadelphia Centennial Exposition does not wonder at the hardihood of a race that could survive in this wilderness, this jungle? Genre painting of the period fills every inch of canvas with something or other; historians

27

of sculpture are hard put to it to distinguish genius in the
age, crowded as genius is by weeping willows in stone,
funerary urns in iron, mausoleums, memorials, and gigantic
and fraudulent façades. As if this were not enough, brick
railway stations pretend to be mediaeval cathedrals, banks are
fronted like the tombs of the Pharaohs, and a business block
imitates a Renaissance palace. I do not dwell upon the various
attachments affixed to female costume. We murmur something about eclecticism, syncretism, exclusiveness for the
masses, but what is all this except the vigorous expression of
endless curiosity, a search into every nook and corner of past
cultures to find out and bring home the triumphs of other
times? Victorian eclecticism has the superabundant energy
of the Baroque, of which, indeed, it is in some sense the heir.

Some part of this eclecticism springs in an upside-down way
from the diminishing centrality of the classical inheritance. Up
to the French Revolution most nations, including Russia,
proudly faced backward to Greece, Rome, and Byzantium,
France acquiring a consulate and the Americans taking on a
senate and a *praesens,* or president. But the restless energy of
the century, expressed as scholarship, as archaeology, as discovery, as anthropology, as commerce, as imperialism steadily
shrunk the sphere of Hellenism, of Roman law, and of the
Judaic tradition. The fateful success of Champollion in
deciphering the Rosetta Stone opened the door to a widen-
ing and deepening of ancient history in Asia, in Africa, and
in the New World. The indebtedness rather than the originality of Greece became a matter of debate, and the excavations
of triumphs of art in the Fertile Crescent, along the Nile, in
Asia Minor, or in Central America diminished the uniqueness
of Hellas and of Israel. Archaeology at Crete or Troy not only
showed that brave men and excessively modern women were
living before Agamemnon and Helen, but that modern
plumbing had been laid on, fifteen hundred years or more
before Christ. Scholarship (it is true, descending from the

eighteenth century) also proclaimed the wisdom of the Hindu, the Chinese, and the Japanese, and discovered other canons of art than those of Sir Joshua Reynolds; and movements of taste, whether labeled romanticism, the quest for the exotic, decadence, primitivism, or the alienation of the artist from society, found virtue in Africa, in subjects from the South Seas, in Japanese prints, in concepts of representation and non-representation that not only had nothing to do with Phidias but that by and by came to prefer archaic Athenian work to the blameless beauty of the age of Praxiteles and its successors. The archaic smile destroyed the spell of Winckelmann. The great century was in truth overwhelmed and embarrassed by the revelation of its cultural inheritances—the cult of the North (as in Wagner's music dramas), the cult of the Slav (as in the vogue of Russian fiction), the cult of the Indian (as in Latin-American poetry and the twentieth–century Dartmouth College Library murals). Classicism was no longer a Golden Milestone. Henry Adams lamented diversity; and though he measured change from his poem to the Virgin and not from the funeral oration of Pericles, he found cultural pluralism characteristic of his time. He must have known: he thought of himself as a child of the eighteenth century.

Attempts to get this kaleidoscopic period into focus have not been lacking. One such is to accuse it of materialism and mercantilism. Tender-minded persons, unhappy before the Rothschilds or the Rockefellers, delineate the age as if the Ruggiero of Ingres' painting somehow failed to come in time to rescue the shrinking Angelica of culture from the bleak rock of bargain-and-sale. They declare that the tremendous triumph of science and invention proved to be a great betrayal of the humane tradition. Science, for them, is materialism; invention supports the internecine warfare of captains of industry. The dreadful thing in the nineteenth century is Hudson the Railway King, the four hundred French families, various German *Aktiengesellschaften,* and the gaudy imitation palaces of Senator Clark and his kind at Newport or along Fifth Avenue. The palaces were certainly built, the ruthlessness existed (read Balzac, or Trollope's *The Way We Live Now*), the materialism is dramatized by the famous Bradley Martin ball.

But this in some measure misreads history by laying emphasis all on one side. It not only forgets the real foundations of the Hanseatic cities and the fortunes of the Medici, the income of the bishopric of Durham and the competition between Venice and Genoa in their palmiest days, it does something less than justice to Senator Clark and his generation. Who supported the Chicago Art Institute? Who gave the National Gallery to the nation? Who created Stanford and the University of Chicago, the Guggenheim Foundation and many another instrument of like kind? God, according to legend, told John D. Rockefeller to give his money to the University of Chicago; in what ways does the revelation differ from that vouchsafed to Jeanne d'Arc or Peter the Hermit? I read in the dispassionate *Encyclopaedia Britannica* that the fifteenth-century Fuggers were "interested in silver mines in Tirol and copper mines in Hungary, while their trade in spices, wool and silk extended to almost all parts of Europe," and I learn that "their wealth enabled them to make large loans to the German king . . . and . . . contributed largely to the election of Charles V. to the imperial throne." Conceivably Mark Hanna and the Duc de Morny are not as original as men believed. Let us try to define the century in some deeper way.

It was, we are told, the century of the middle class. The middle class eventually captured the French Revolution and sustained the control of revolutions at least until 1917. The beerage married the peerage. The *haute bourgeoisie* turned out the Bourbons and brought in the Citizen King. In Germany, the Zollverein proved to be the practical expression of middle-class philosophy—read Pfizer's *Briefwechsel zweier Deutschen*

30

and learn how the Hohenzollerns are miraculously burgher kings, or at least potentially so. And the supposition that the nineteenth century is *par excellence* the era of the middle class receives indirect and emphatic support in the scorn of Byron Gautier, Flaubert, Ibsen, and, *mirabile dictu,* William Dean Howells, for the unfortunate and unenlightened taste of the bourgeoisie.

But softly, softly. The historic duty of the middle class is to be always rising. It was rising in the eighteenth century— witness sentimental comedy and the theories of Diderot. It was rising in the seventeenth century—hence the overthrow of Charles I. It was rising in the Elizabethan period—read Louis Wright's book on middle-class culture in that same Elizabethan age. It was rising in Henry VIII's time—hence the despoliation of the monasteries and, elsewhere, the interest of "adventurers" in America. We have just seen it rising in the case of the fifteenth-century Fugger family. I read that in Europe vernacular drama was occasioned by the prosperity of the guilds, those distinctive expressions of a rising middle class. It is, of course, theoretically possible that this perpetual rising reached its climax in Victoria's jubilee of 1887, but as I also learn that the predicament of the American labor movement is that it is today essentially and hopelessly enamored of middle-class comfort, I am not persuaded that the many middle-class characteristics of the nineteenth century notably distinguish it from centuries before and since its time.

Historians rightly make much of the nation-state and the rivalries of nationalism, racism, and imperialism as part of the foundations of the nineteenth century. The facts are undeniable. The French Revolution in a sense created the very peoples it sought to liberate; and the romantic movement, by its appeals to racial pasts so vague that they were malleable (in the Balkans, if there was no local Homer, national epics were obligingly manufactured), was to lure nations into thinking with their blood. Unification movements in Italy and

Germany are there for all men to see; and in the name of race or folk or nation or patriotism the world grew increasingly fragmentary as Holland and Belgium split, the Scandinavias became independent states, Iceland broke off from Denmark, succession states in the old Austro-Hungarian empire made the map look like a bed quilt, and in Latin America colonies set up in business for themselves. Young Germany, young Italy, young England (there was even a young America movement!)—these are familiar emotional drives. Nineteenth-century imperialism carried with it the seeds of its own destruction; and as nations continue to proliferate, it is a nice question whether the planners have left enough space for flagpoles on a certain plaza in New York City.

The concept is crucial for an understanding of the age, but it must not be pushed too far. There were nation-states before 1789. Racial and national hatreds, alas, are no invention of the age of Vater Jahn and Houston Stewart Chamberlain. Consider the contempt of a sound eighteenth-century English lad for a nation of "mounseers" and frogeaters, the hatred of the Dutch sea beggar for Catholic Spain, the terror of the West before Islam, the shiver of Elizabethans at the thought of those slippery people, the Renaissance Italians, the enthusiasm with which Burgundians slaughtered Frenchmen, Swedes massacred Germans, and Poles carried fire and sword into Russia, the Ukraine, and, for that matter, into Poland during centuries of history that are a little dim to our high-school–trained eyes. It is true that the organization of the mediaeval university into "nations" was a matter of law and lodging, but it should not escape the reader that turbulence in Bologna or Paris was more commonly between "nations" than within any one of them. The point is not to deny the tremendous economic importance of the consolidation of nations between 1789 and 1917; the point is to see that the bitterness of man for man is nothing novel, nothing strange.

Is it possible to look further? I believe it is, and tentatively

32

advance for discussion four characteristics of this great time. If in so doing I have unwittingly stolen the thunder of anyone else, I apologize in the name of our common enthusiasms. I suggest that one important component of the nineteenth century is the attempt at the Europeanization of the globe; a second is the increasing resort to violence as a mode of securing change in government; a third is the substitution of a dynamic theory of nature for a mechanical explanation; and a fourth is the universalization of mathematics and the increasing application of mathematics to culture.

At the opening of the century most of Africa, Australia, the Pacific Ocean, and much of North and South America and Asia were still "unknown." At the close of the century all the continents and all the seas were "known," and by 1909 the North Pole had been reached, by 1911 the South. Exploration was thereafter to be confined to high mountains, the depths of the sea, and the illimitable air. This expression of nineteenth-century energy is principally the work of Europeans and their derivatives, the North Americans; and by the end of the century the white race, as somebody has pointed out, had been thrown into contact with every non-white people on the face of the earth. Is not this at least as remarkable as the Hellenization of the world by Alexander and his successors?

The natures of these contacts were many, but one can usefully distinguish three, each with its crucial cultural implications. One is obviously the missionary movement, or the attempt to convert the world to a Europeanized version of Christianity—no invention of the time, but a movement increasingly systematized and rationalized as salvation and hymn-singing gave way to schools and medical missions. A second is, of course, the attempt, not at religious domination, but at political domination, either by colonization and settlement or by conquest and annexation or by the creation of spheres of influence. A third, flowing from the other two, is the effort at "modernization"—that is, Europeanization of "inferior" racial stocks and alien cultures, a movement prodigious alike for good and for harm. The good intentions of a Macaulay imposing British law on the sub-continent of India as an offset to the rapacity of the East India Company are one thing; the "modernization" of non-European armies—that is, the spread of destructive weapons around the globe—is another. Intricate questions of interpretation arise as one balances health programs, improvement in the status of women, modernization of agriculture, the spread of education, and the like great values against the economic exploitation of backward peoples, the blotting out of local or regional cultures, and other deleterious effects. All this is perhaps obvious, but when, since the attempt of Islam to cover the earth, has one culture impinged so rapidly, so violently, and perhaps so successfully upon all the others?

Modernization, we are accustomed to say, reduces time and space, the globe shrinks, the continents jostle each other, and tensions and understandings alike appear in new and changing contexts. Perhaps the century that sent Macaulay to India on a voyage that consumed four months but got Phileas Fogg around the world in eighty days could not understand that it was also creating impatience; and in politics the nineteenth century might be dubbed the age of impatience, the expression of which is revolution. Bemused as we are by Victorian stability, we do not see that the British story is almost unique in a century that increasingly turned to revolution as a normal political instrument. Through the century France exhibits what Wordsworth divined as early as 1802—that is, unceasing change; from 1800 to 1900 it moved from a consulate to an empire to the Bourbon monarchy to the Orleans monarchy to the second republic to the second empire to the third republic. Nor is France sole, though it may be singular, in this regard. Violence convulses this or that area or nation in Africa, Asia, and the Americas. There were colonial revolts in the Turkish empire, in India, in the Spanish empire, in

Canada, in South Africa, to name only the most important. There were civil wars in Spain, in the United States, in Latin America, in China, in Japan. The transmogrifications of governments in the Italian peninsula are as remarkable as those in France, and so likewise are those in the Balkans. It is difficult to number and assess assassinations in history, but, considering attempts on the lives of nineteenth-century rulers from Napoleon to McKinley, one might reasonably make the revolver and the bomb no less than the ballot box and parliamentary government symbols of its public life. We have to go back to the Renaissance to parallel this restlessness, this amoral energy, this glittering combination of appeals to legal processes and resort to unlawful combinations and lawless means.

As if to find sanction in the cosmos for its terrible strength, the nineteenth century profoundly altered the theory of nature from a mechanical explanation to a dynamic one. The Newtonian world, as somebody has said, may be likened to a smoothly purring machine planned, executed, and superintended by an infinite engineer.

> Nature, and Nature's laws, lay hid in night;
> God said, Let Newton Be! And there was Light,

we read, just as we read in Addison's famous hymn:

> What though, in solemn silence, all
> Move round the dark, terrestrial ball?
>
> . . . .
>
> In reason's ear they all rejoice,
> And utter forth a glorious voice,
> For ever singing as they shine,
> The hand that made us is divine.

Divinity was frictionless harmony; and Addison's poem, attached to a *Spectator* paper of 1712, was supposed to demonstrate that the perfection of this harmony could be evident only through contemplation—one must be "out of the noise

35

and hurry of human affairs." The age of Goethe and Darwin, of Liebig and Thomas Edison could not thus separate human affairs from the contemplaton of cosmic harmonies. Human affairs were part of the cosmos, part of the hurry and bustle, the conflict and collision of the universe. So it is that Faust, that supreme expression of nineteenth-century man, summons up the Earth Spirit only to be appalled and fascinated by him:

GEIST: Wer ruft mir?

FAUST (*abgewendet*): Schreckliches Gesicht!

GEIST: Du has mich mächtig angezogen,
    An meiner Sphäre lang' gesogen,
    Und nun—

FAUST: Weh! ich ertrag' dich nicht!

GEIST: Du flehst eratmend, mich zu schauen,
    Meine Stimme zu hören, mein Antlitz zu sehn;
    Mich neigt dein mächtig Seelenflehn,
    Da bin ich!—Welch erbärmlich Grauen
    Fasst übermenschen dich! Wo ist der Seele Ruf?
    Wo ist die Brust, die eine Welt in sich erschuf
    Und trug and hegte, die mit Freudebeben
    Erschwoll, sich uns, den Geistern, gleich zu heben?
    Wo bist du, Faust, des Stimme mir erklang,
    Der sich an mich mit allen Kräften drang?
    Bist du es, der, von meinem Hauch umwittert,
    In allen Lebenstiefen zittert,
    Ein furchtsam weggekrümmter Wurm?

FAUST: Soll ich dir, Flammenbildung, weichen?
    Ich bin's, bin Faust, bin deinesgleichen!

GEIST: In Lebensfluten, im Tatensturm
    Wall' ich auf und ab,
    Webe hin und her!
    Geburt und Grab,
    Ein ewiges Meer,
    Ein wechselnd Weben,
    Ein glühend Leben,
    So schaff' ich am sausenden Webstuhl der Zeit
    Und wirke der Gottheit lebendiges Kleid.

FAUST: Der du die weite Welt umschweifst,
    Geschäftiger Geist, wie nah fühl' ich mich dir!

GEIST: Du gleichst dem Geist, den du begreifst,
Nicht mir! *(Verschwindet)*[1]

Goethe is frequently tedious, but nothing in his work more clearly validates his claim to genius than this scene in *Faust,* where, with prophetic insight, he foretells the dilemma of nineteenth-century thought confronting the science of which nineteenth-century thought is both the creator and the creation. Theories of development, theories of evolution, the mysterious doctrine of entropy, the reformulation of the astronomical problems from the time of the Herschels to Ritchey's identification in 1917 of a nova in the Great Spiral Nebula in Andromeda—these are, as it were, gigantic commentaries upon the dialogue between the Spirit and Faust.[2] The paradox is brilliantly expressed in an epigram about astronomy. Astronomy reduces man to total insignificance in a universe that cares nothing about him, but it is man the astronomer who has discovered and is exploring this universe. If nineteenth-century readers might have agreed with Shelley that

[1] The Bayard Taylor translation:
SPIRIT: Who calls me? FAUST (*with averted head*): Terrible to see! SPIRIT: Me hast thou long with might attracted, / Long from my sphere thy food exacted, / And now— FAUST: Woe! I endure not thee! SPIRIT: To view me is thine aspiration, / My voice to hear, my countenance to see; / Thy powerful yearning moveth me, / Here am I!—what mean perturbation / Thee, superhuman, shakes? Thy soul's high calling, where? / Where is the breast, which from itself a world did bear, / And shaped and cherished —which with joy expanded, / To be our peer, with us, the Spirits, banded? / Where art thou, Faust, whose voice has pierced to me, / Who towards me pressed with all thine energy? / *He* art thou, who, my presence breathing, seeing, / Trembles through all the depths of being, / A writhing worm, a terror-stricken form? FAUST: Thee, form of flame, shall I then fear? / Yes, I am Faust: I am thy peer! SPIRIT: In the tides of Life, in Action's storm, / A fluctuant wave, / A shuttle free, / Birth and the Grave, / An eternal sea, / A weaving, flowing / Life, all-glowing, / Thus at Time's humming loom 't is my hand prepares / The garment of Life which the Deity wears! FAUST: Thou, who around the wide world wendest, / Thou busy Spirit, how near I feel to thee! SPIRIT: Thou'rt like the Spirit which thou comprehendest, / Not me! (*Disappears.*)
[2] See in this connection the wonderful series of articles on modern theories of the universe in the *Scientific American,* September, 1956.

37

> Worlds on worlds are rolling ever
> From creation to decay,
> Like the bubbles on a river
> Sparkling, bursting, borne away,

nobody in 1917 could have accepted Shelley's inference of 1821 that therefore

> The world's great age begins anew
> The golden years return.

The fourth characteristic common to nineteenth-century culture I have called the universalization and utilization of mathematics, an area in which the layman is helpless except as he notes and muses upon the results. He notes how, beginning with Gauss's *Disquisitiones arithmeticae* of 1801, mathematical analysis of all sorts has moved steadily into greater complexity and greater uncertainty, so that today, after the conclusion of the nineteenth century, Dantzig, in his influential *Number: The Language of Science,* can say:

Mathematics and experiment reign more firmly than ever over the new physics, but an all-pervading scepticism has affected their validity. Man's confident belief in the absolute validity of the two methods has been found to be of an anthropomorphic origin; both have been found to rest on articles of faith.

Mathematics would collapse like a house of cards were it deprived of the certainties that man may safely proceed as though he possessed an unlimited memory, and an inexhaustible life lay ahead of him. It is on this assumption that the validity of infinite processes is based, and these processes dominate mathematical analysis . . . arithmetic itself would lose its generality were this hypothesis refuted, for our concept of whole number is inseparable from it; and so would geometry and mechanics. This catastrophe would in turn uproot the whole edifice of the physical sciences.

Yet, though the validity of inference, to go on with Dantzig, may rest on "no firmer foundation than the human longing for certainty and permanence," mathematics has become the universal language of mankind—a triumph of the nineteenth century *par excellence.* Moreover, whatever metaphysical doubts may haunt experts, mathematics enchain the ordinary man as neither Renaissance tyranny nor an absolute monarchy could do. The exact sciences aside, the unique contribution of the pragmatic nineteenth century here was the perfecting of statistical analysis, notably in questions of public policy. Western man is no longer Byronic or Faustian; the nineteenth century eventually reduced him to an integer, a unit, a faceless atom, a nameless one in a myriad of other nameless ones. He lives in a tangle of numerical systems—a numbered house, a numbered license card, a numbered marriage certificate, a numbered tax receipt, a numbered grave. His opinions are calculable in a poll, but they are no longer "his" opinions; they are simply an infinitesimal in an indefinite series. A calculating machine confronts him at the bank, at a turnstile, when he weighs himself, when he faces a health examiner, when he writes an examination. His expectations of life, the rate he will pay for insurance, his capacity to contribute to the support of the state, his capacity to retire from business at any given age, the probability of his voting pro or con, and the possibility of his response to this kind of advertising rather than that—by the end of the nineteenth century these and other aspects of individualism were being reduced by curve and graph, median and mean, sample and extrapolation, to the anonymity of twentieth-century culture. If the great triumph of nineteenth-century research has been that it learned to measure change and to induce change in order that it may be measured, the more ambiguous success of that period was to create a mensurative culture in which personalities were reduced to persons, in which the populace replaced the people. The science of statistics, despite some precedents essentially a nineteenth-century invention, may in the long run be that against which men shall revolt in vain.

But the true greatness of the nineteenth century is no more to be adjudged by the potential misuses of its mathematical discoveries than the *expertise* of Pope is to be estimated by the preface to the *Lyrical Ballads*. Its greatness lies in its astonishing achievements in science, in education, in the arts. Take, as a single instance, the arts. The nineteenth century is the classic century of the novel, the literary form that is to modernity what epic poetry was to earlier epochs. One thinks at once of Scott, Balzac, Dickens, Turgenev, Manzoni, Zola, Flaubert, Tolstoi, Dostoevski, Hawthorne, James, and a thousand more. In *Faust* it contributed to world literature a great philosophic poem, and in *Don Juan* of Byron the greatest comic epic in history; but one has no sooner singled out Goethe and Byron than other poets come forward by the score for recognition—Wordsworth, Pushkin, Heine, Leopardi, Hugo, Baudelaire, Tennyson, Whitman, and their peers. Granted that the seeds of any large movement in art are sown well in advance, granted also that parallels and prophecies are soon found for any change, the century is distinguished for at least four great and profound doctrines of art—romanticism, realism, naturalism, and symbolism, and for such offshoots as the art-for-art's-sake movement. Its historians are equally impressive, from Niebuhr to Henry Adams, and the roll of its critics includes such names as Sainte-Beuve, Arnold, Croce, and Burckhardt. In painting it produced impressionism and the whole "modern phase," nor are its black-and-white work, its water colors, its posters, and its caricatures less than brilliant. In music what variety and range! *Otello, Falstaff, Carmen, Tristan und Isolde, Louise,* the *Symphonie fantastique,* the *Rhenish Symphony,* the symphonies of Brahms, the *Lieder* of Schubert, the song-cycles of Schumann, the Viennese waltz, Gilbert and Sullivan, Offenbach, *Der Zigeunerbaron,* all enclosed, as it were, between the *Fifth Symphony* and *Der Rosenkavalier!* But the mind begins by and by to tire and to rebel against this catalog of grandeur.

Whether these speculations have merit or not, there remains the problem of nineteenth-century style. All great cultural epochs have their styles; and some are content to dismiss that of the nineteenth century as mere eclecticism, a function of commerce and archaeology. Surely, however, few mistake nineteenth-century work of any sort for the work of any other cultural epoch. The restlessness of this immense period, the wide-ranging curiosity of its mighty geniuses, the very revolutionary fervor that distinguishes much of it—these could not rest in mere eclecticism, in plumage borrowed from other times. Alexandrianism appears in the nineteenth century, but the nineteenth century is not Alexandrian. I should rather contend that fullness of expression, amplitude, an exhaustless treasure of resources is characteristic of nineteenth-century style. Eighteenth-century style is referable to common centers and common canons of taste; not so with its successor. It is never content with austerity. Painting, opera, symphonic music, piano compositions, architecture, literature, oratory—everywhere one finds, it seems to me, the same dynamism and flow, the same aspiration and abundance. Consider the prose of Balzac, Emerson, Dickens, Hugo, and Ruskin, the music of Wagner, Musorgski, and Richard Strauss, the cartoons of Gavarni, Daumier, Nast, and Tenniel—everywhere fullness of detail, the same lively curiosity, as if nothing had been written or composed or drawn in the world before. The "note" of Victorian literature, according to Oliver Elton, is nobility; I would amend this for the total epoch and declare that the general "note" of nineteenth-century style is restless aspiration. The century of the skyscraper comes as close to heaven, in one sense, as the century of the Strassburg cathedral, and if the cathedral according to romantic theory, yearns for the infinite, the skyscraper may be fairly said to yearn for power.

Everywhere, in sum, energy: energy that, if it exhausts itself, expresses its exhaustion with a kind of patient fury, as in Schopenhauer, or else lingers with delight over its own decay, as in Swinburne, Baudelaire, Huysmans, and Oscar Wilde.

But we do wrong to consider the aesthetes and the decadents too seriously. Sir Kenneth Clark, commenting on a self-portrait by Leonardo da Vinci, writes as follows:

This great furrowed mountain of a face with its noble brow, commanding cavernous eyes and undulating foothills of beard is like the faces of all the great men of the nineteenth century as the camera has perserved them for us—Darwin, Tolstoy, Walt Whitman. Time, with its spectacle of human suffering has reduced them all to a common level of venerability.

This is well observed, except that I would have said "raised" rather than "reduced."

The Generation of 1830

An address at the opening of an exhibition of books and manuscripts, "From Poet to Premier: 1809 and After," held at the Grolier Club in New York during February and March, 1959. The exhibit consisted principally of the writings of important personages of the English-speaking world who were born in 1809. Previously published in *Harvard Library Bulletin,* Vol. XIII (Autumn 1959), 400–414.

I F WE accept the canonical legal theory that at twenty-one men arrive at years of indiscretion, then we may call the group born in 1809—the year of Gladstone's birth—the generation of 1830. Confining ourselves to some leading names, we note that though Poe's *Tamerlane* appeared in 1827, the *Al Aaraaf* volume of 1829 is better poetry. Holmes printed his "Old Ironsides" poem in 1830 and began *The Autocrat of the Breakfast Table* in a magazine of 1831. Tennyson's 1830 book, *Poems, Chiefly Lyrical,* clearly announced a new genius. Gladstone's speech of May, 1831, before the Oxford Union was called the most eloquent ever delivered before that society and proclaimed his oratorical powers. In December, 1831, Darwin departed on the *Beagle* to explore the Galapàgos Islands and the ideas of Lyell's new *Principles of Geology.* Of the better known names only Fitzgerald and Lincoln were late in maturing. The leading dates fall conveniently around 1830, and we may therefore attempt to place this generation in history.

In 1830 George IV went to his dubious award, to be succeeded by King William, derisively known as Silly Billy, who, however, had sense enough to force a recalcitrant House of

43

Lords to accept the Reform Bill of 1832, which in fact inaugurated the Victorian world. (Victoria, by the by, in 1830 was eleven, going on twelve.) Across the channel Louis Philippe and his umbrella were similarly inaugurating the kingdom of the middle class. Over the rest of Europe the spirit and policy of Metternich prevailed, that Metternich who had written his wife some years earlier: "I have become a species of moral power." In Russia a new czar was simultaneously liberating Greece and closing down on the universities, wherein earnest young Hegelians were discovering mystical virtues in autocracy, slavophilism, and Holy Russia. In the United States a former professor of rhetoric and oratory at Harvard, by name John Quincy Adams, was planning to devote himself to his books, while in the White House, Andrew Jackson personified the rude vigor of an ebullient class hard to define save that it was not revolutionary and was bourgeois in its values.

Except in France, the year 1830 marks the twilight of romanticism. In Great Britain Byron, Shelley, and Keats were dead, Wordsworth was past his prime, and in two years, worn out by incessant writing, the Wizard of the North was to die. In the United States of 1830, Channing printed his once celebrated "Remarks on National Literature," Audubon had begun his *Birds of America,* Webster replied to Hayne, and Mrs. Sarah Josepha Hale published a poem to be set to music by Lowell Mason which begins:

> Mary had a little lamb,
> Its fleece was white as snow.

The poem denies the Calvinistic doctrine that children are mere limbs of Satan and is in that sense romantic, just as Webster's oration and Channing's essay partake of romantic nationalism and Audubon's birds partake of romantic nature. But the generation of 1830 faces both ways, and so Mrs. Hale's poem also anticipates the Kate Greenaway books, Channing merely sketches what Emerson, Whitman, and William Dean

Howells are later to affirm, and Webster's oration foreshadows the strong nationalists and the economic imperialism of the later century. Let us return briefly to Europe.

The year of Scott's death was also the year when Goethe died after completing *Faust*. Goethe is sometimes regarded as the first modern man, and the Faustian spirit is supposed by philosophers like Spengler to symbolize modernity. Certainly by 1832 the German romantics were gone or going, just as in Russia in 1832 the publication of the last part of Pushkin's *Evgenii Onegin* marks the culmination and the decline of romanticism. Even in France, where Gautier's waistcoat flamed like a banner at every riotous performance of Hugo's *Hernani,* a young man named Balzac had begun his serious literary career in 1829, an old man called Stendhal published *Le Rouge et le Noir* in 1830, and a German Jew, officially described as "blasphemous, indecent, subversive, and replete with *lése majesté,*" fled from Germany to Paris in 1831. Of him Matthew Arnold was later to write:

> The Spirit of the world,
> Beholding the absurdity of men—
> Their vaunts, their feats—let a sardonic smile
> For one short moment, wander o'er his lips.
> *That smile was Heine!*

Heine, too, retains his romantic traits, but he is essentially a modernist, somebody far closer to T. S. Eliot than he is to Percy Bysshe Shelley. The cultural world of 1830 was evidently split down the middle, and a fading romanticism was trying to come to terms with a new something nobody could quite define. It was not realism, not naturalism—these were to come in the second half of this amazing epoch—it was something for which we have no good name. It was too early for Victorianism, or for General Grant, or for Eastlake furniture (though Eastlake became an R.A. in 1830), and it was obviously too early for Prince Albert, who was not born until 1819. Let us call it seriousness.

Seriousness was a somewhat complicated matter. All these young men, born in 1809, the year of Wagram, when the Napoleonic empire was at its height, could later understand the significance of Musset's brilliant and melancholy novel, *La Confession d'un enfant du siècle,* the hero of which, young, pale, embittered, was, he tells us, conceived between two battles and born to the sound of cannon. When they reached their majority, the long nightmare of the French Revolution and the dictatorship of Napoleon lay in the past of these young orators and poets, these scientists and translators, but the contemporary world of Metternich did not inspirit them, it did not strengthen them. The popular revolts of 1830—did they perchance portend more carnage, another world war? Or were they the dawn of an era of peace and of the people? The young men could not then, or later, make up their minds. Tennyson went to Spain to find out, but not many years after, fearful of the populace, he referred condescendingly to "the red foolfury of the Seine." On the other hand, Lincoln, his contemporary, was to declare that government of the people, for the people, and by the people shall not perish from the earth. Were you for or against humanity, that humanity Michelet, whose *Introduction à l'histoire universelle* appeared in 1831, turned into an earthly god? To escape from the dilemma, Holmes, the Brahmin, retreated into the eighteenth century, whereas Poe, his strange contemporary, in "Mellonta Tauta," a tale of the year 2848, painted a gloomy picture of democracy. Fitzgerald managed to maintain a genial scepticism about humanity, and Darwin educed man from the animal kingdom. In his old age, of course, Gladstone could refer to the "God-fearing and God-sustaining University of Oxford," and is nowadays thought of as somebody who achieved the whole and perfect liberal faith in man. Certainly he believed that even fallen women, that even members of the Greek Orthodox Church, could be redeemed, and he died a great Christian statesman, as Lord Salisbury said. Lord Salisbury was a devout Anglican, who ought to know. But Gladstone, too, was throughout his life a split personality, an Italian in the grip of a Scotsman, says one biographer, a being divided, says another, who finds two Gladstones—one, "Mr. Liverpool," the shrewd, ambitious politician, the other, "Mr. Oxford," the High Churchman with leanings towards celibacy and recondite theological arguments.

To most of us, these early Victorians and Victorian Americans look as strong and substantial as their own daguerreotypes, but what the French call the malady of the century was nevertheless common to them—to Poe, the psychiatric; to Gladstone, the divided man; to Tennyson, whose *In Memoriam* is not so much a cry for faith as a desperate struggle to fight off hallucination; to Lincoln, who suffered from melancholia; to Darwin, whose perpetual ill health was psychosomatic; to Fitzgerald, whose Omar Khayyam offers a conclusion in which nothing is concluded; even to Oliver Wendell Holmes, who could never quite make up his mind whether sin is a moral fact or a biological stain. "If, on presentation of the evidence," he wrote of Elsie Venner in 1883, "she becomes by the verdict of the human conscience a proper object of divine pity, and not of divine wrath, as a subject of moral poisoning, wherein lies the difference between her position at the bar of judgment, human or divine, and that of the unfortunate victim who received a moral poison from a remote ancestor before he drew his first breath?" Wherein, indeed? This looks as if, in repudiating Calvinism, Holmes had made up his mind on one of the great moral issues of his age; but at the end of the novel, Elsie dies as much the victim of the plot as if she had been either a deist or a Borgia. Holmes too was a divided man.

Of course every generation regards its own era as filled with sick hurry and divided aims. Because of their autobiographical and confessional habits, because they lived in an age when the papers of great men were conscientiously preserved—John Morley, Gladstone's biographer, estimates that "between two

47

and three hundred thousand written papers of one sort or another" passed through his hands—we know more about the generation of 1830 than we know about the generation of Shakespeare or of Dante or of Boethius or of Sophocles. But the habit of confusion is at least as old as the Tower of Babel. If they had had the confessional drive and the scholarly training of modernity, writers who contributed books to the library of Ashurbanipal might also now be proved to be proper subjects for Freudian analysis. These cautionary speculations, though doubtless valuable, do not alter the historic truth that the men of 1809, the generation of 1830, were in fact troubled men, living in troubled times, as, indeed, the phrase "Victorian Compromise" itself attests. You do not compromise issues unless the forces on either hand are virtually equal. The great issues of mankind, as Judge Learned Hand has observed, are never solved, they are merely ignored. The great issues of 1830 are in that sense still before us.

But it is not thus that we commonly think of the world of the nineteenth century. Those, we say, were simpler times. Would that we could return to them! Standards were fixed, values secure, diplomacy leisurely, wars minor, business simpler (being without social security or complicated taxes), politics responsible, domesticity not only commonplace but rampant, the colonies knew their places, and so did servants, women, and labor, and heaven was so immediate that Gladstone could write without embarrassment after having attended the burial of Lady Canning, "May we live as by the side of a grave and looking in." Said Tennyson solemnly: "We cannot live in art alone," and he wrote "The Palace of Art" to prove it, a poem in which works of art are so enduringly described we do not in the least care that the tenant of the palace is finally driven to inhabit a cottage in the vale, a remove that seems to us nowadays mainly to exhibit a puzzling taste in real estate. Though Tennyson once said that "the general English view of God is as of an immeasurable clergyman;

and some mistake the devil for God," we feel that the Victorian world is better expressed in another statement of his: "There are moments when the flesh is nothing to me, when I feel and know the flesh to be the vision, God and the Spiritual the only real and true." Why, then, this queer contradiction between our impression of the early Victorian world—or all of it, for that matter—as something simple and substantial, comfortable and kind; and the historical truth that its leading men were perpetually torn between purposes? How reconcile, so to speak, the Tennyson who wrote "The Two Voices," an agonized debate between faith and doubt, and the Tennyson who wrote *The Idylls of the King?* Why do we have this impresson of solidity from an age of tensions?

Every age has its own special resonance. We cannot translate eighteenth-century writing into any other style. We know at once what baroque painting, what baroque architecture, what baroque costumes truly are. You cannot substitute the words of Dickens for the words of Malory any more than you can mistake beer for brandy. Each cultural epoch has its own pace, its own rhythm, its own pattern of stereotype and response. Words remain as formal elements spelled out; their connotation and denotation are as a flowing river. When in *Twelfth Night* Maria says of this disguised Viola that he is now in some commerce with my lady, she means one thing; when Milton talks about looks commercing with the skies, he means something else; when the founding fathers gave Congress the right to regulate commerce, they meant a third thing; and our modern chambers of commerce have virtually little or nothing to do with any of the three earlier meanings of the term. The problem is not merely one of looking up definitions in a dictionary; the problem is one of weight and onset in a word, a sentence, the organization of a paragraph, the purposes of title-pages, the attitude of writer towards reader and of reader towards writer, just as in iconography and iconology, though the naive spectator can enumerate the objects in a painting, it requires a cultural expert to tell us what they mean and why they are there.

But it takes time to establish what I have called the resonance, and what others may prefer to call the style, of any age. Obviously, the deeper the perspective in time, the easier, in one sense, it becomes to determine the primary characteristics of historical styles. It is relatively easy to identify Minoan pottery; it is relatively difficult to differentiate the stylistic qualities of a novel published in 1890 from those of a novel published fifty years later. You can, as I say, in virtually every case distinguish eighteenth-century writing from every other sort of writing, but it is hard to determine the temporal provenience of nineteenth-century work. From what part of the century does the following passage derive?

Genius, however, he certainly possessed, and genius of high order. His ardent, tender, and magnificent turn of thought, his brilliant fancy, his command of expression, at once forcible and elegant, must be acknowledged. Nature meant him for the prince of lyric writers. But by one fatal present she deprived her other gifts of half their value. . . . The honey of sensuous description is spread so deeply over the surface of the goblet that a large proportion of its readers never think of its holding anything else. All the phases of unhallowed passion are described in full detail.

I have, of course, indulged in trickery. The first part of this paragraph is from Macaulay's "Petrarch," printed in 1824, and the second is from Holmes's *Over the Teacups,* published in 1891, almost seventy years later. Holmes is denouncing *Madame Bovary,* Macaulay is about to demonstrate the paucity of Petrarch's thought, and I perform my little feat of legerdemain not as a trick but as a warning to myself to be cautious in what I am about to say concerning seriousness in the nineteenth century.

Nevertheless something must be said; and unfortunately the first thing that has to be said is that because of the decaying interest in stylistic analysis among nineteenth-century scholars, nobody nowadays says anything much about the problem. We once used to take apart the paragraphs of Macaulay; but today the same amount of energy is expended in hunting down symbolism in the prose of Melville, an enterprise that, whatever it may do for an understanding of *Moby-Dick,* does very little for an objective study of style. Since, however, discussions of sentence length, diction, parallelism, and the like components of rhetoric are not in themselves exciting topics for discourse, one may be grateful that so far as the nineteenth century is concerned, this kind of information is feeble or lacking, a fact that forces me into generalizations that cannot be supported by statistical evidence. What impression does nineteenth-century writing make on the sensitive reader? What can be usefully said of this tension between a fading romanticism and a mounting seriousness in the generation of 1830? Why is it, when most of them were provably suffering from the malady of the century—that is, from the uncertainty of divided aims—their work yet leaves on readers this profound impression of solidity, assurance, depth, and strength?

Let us put in contrast a pair of representative selections in prose and another pair in verse, placing in each bracket one piece from the writings of the men of 1830 and one from living writers. Here is a poem written by a man born in 1809:

Nightingales warbled without,
   Within was weeping for thee;
Shadows of three dead men
   Walk'd in the walks with me,
   Shadows of three dead men, and thou wast one of the three.
Nightingales sang in his woods,
   The Master was far away;
Nightingales warbled and sang
   Of a passion that lasts but a day;
   Still in the house in his coffin the Prince of courtesy lay.
Two dead men have I known
   In courtesy like to thee;

Two dead men have I loved
    With a love that ever will be;
    Three dead men have I loved, and thou art last of the three.

This poem is by Alfred Tennyson, it was written in 1870, and it was occasioned by Tennyson's grief for the death of Sir John Simeon, the owner of Swainston and a particular friend of the poet. The other two dead men are Henry Lushington, to whom Tennyson dedicated *The Princess,* and Arthur Hallam. To me, in its classical restraint, its concentration, its simplicity, it is a rather moving if somewhat mannered poem. Whatever one may think of it, one has, I think, no difficulty in understanding it. The poet, accompanied as it were by the ghosts of three dead friends, walks in a garden while the nightingales sing their brief songs of transient passion, and he remembers his lasting love for three shadows, one of whom, newly dead, had been in life the owner of the garden where the poet meditates.

Let me now set beside this lyric another, modern poem also trafficking in memory and nostalgia, a poem quite as good as Tennyson's—perhaps in the opinion of contemporaries even better. It is by Conrad Aiken, and here it is:

This image or another, this quick choosing,
raindrop choosing a path through grains of sand
the blood-drop choosing its way, that the dead world
may wake and think or sleep and dream

This gesture or another, this quick action
the bough broken by the wind and flung down
the hand striking or touching, that the dead world
may know itself and forget itself

This memory or another, this brief picture
sunbeam on the shrivelled and frosted leaf
a world of selves trying to remember the self
before the idea of self is lost—

Walk with me world, upon my right hand walk
speak to me Babel, that I may strive to assemble
of all these syllables a single word
before the purpose of speech is gone.

This is from Mr. Aiken's volume, *Time in the Rock: Preludes to Definition,* published in 1936, a little more than sixty years after Tennyson's poem was published in 1874. What is one to make of it?

Well, three things seem immediately manifest. First, in Mr. Aiken's poem somebody is walking somewhere, he is not sure of himself, he is a very transient being, and he is so convinced of his own fugitive quality that he implores something called the world and something else called Babel to walk or speak with him in order that he may compose with their help "a single word," by which he may mean either this poem or some coherent expression of something else before "the purpose of speech is gone." Second, this poem seems to have something obscurely to do with a parallel between actions in the physical world—raindrops choosing a path, blood-drops choosing a way, boughs broken by the wind, sunbeams striking on a frosted leaf—and the concept of the self—myself, yourself, the poet's self, anybody's self. Third, as in Tennyson's poem, the poet is talking to himself and is overheard by the reader; but unlike Tennyson's poem, this overheard poem is rather difficult to understand. In Tennyson's poem the poet, though he speaks a little enigmatically, speaks in the ordinary language and syntax of a man talking to men. But in Aiken's poem the reader, not the poet, is expected to do all the work; the reader is expected to equate the opening phrase about this image or another with the parallel of the raindrop, the blood-drop, the broken bough, and the sunlit frosted leaf and the action of the mind remembering yesterday and striving to put into words the significance of yesterday, of confusion, of the interrelations of the outer world and the inner world and of the difficulties in this relation wih reference to speech and therefore to life and therefore to the art of speaking, the art of poetry. There can be no doubt that Aiken's poem is the more profound and subtle one, but there can be little doubt also that it is the more obscure and difficult poem, so difficult, indeed, that one might apply to it a scornful phrase about poets talking to themselves. Tennyson tacitly assumes a responsibility for public diction and syntax, and fulfills it; Conrad Aiken tacitly assumes he has a right to make the reader work at the poem until he, the reader, has arrived, so to speak, at the private meaning concealed in its tantalizing and beautiful lines.

Let me now take two parallel examples from prose, each by a leader of his nation. The first is from a speech by Gladstone delivered in 1877—the same decade as that of Tennyson's poem —on the Russo-Turkish War, an event fraught with peril for the peace of Europe, an event in which Gladstone was in the minority and therefore on the losing side. Here is the passage:

> It is not yet too late, I say, to become competitors for that prize; but be assured that whether you meant to claim for yourselves even a single leaf in that immortal chaplet of renown, which will be the reward of true labour in that cause, or whether you turn your backs upon that cause and your own duty, I believe, for one, that the knell of Turkish tyranny in those provinces has sounded.[1]

I turn for my modern example to a speech by the President of the United States delivered on 9 January, 1959, which has at least these parallels: the speaker, like Gladstone, belongs to the minority party and is therefore on the losing side; and, like Gladstone, he is speaking in a period of tension—the cold war with Russia—believed to be of peril to the peace of the world. The following sentences are representative:

> Now these few highlights point up our steady military gains. We are rightfully gratified by the achievements they represent. But we must remember that these imposing armaments are purchased at great cost.

[1] *Hansard's Parliamentary Debates,* 3rd ser., CCXXXIV (London, 1877), col. 439.

54

National security programs account for nearly 60 per cent of the entire Federal budget for this coming fiscal year.

Modern weapons are exceedingly expensive.[2]

No one, I take it, can misunderstand Mr. Eisenhower's meaning. But what a world of difference in cultural weight lies between the cadence, diction, and economy of Gladstone's prose and the cadence, diction, and economy of the prose of Mr. Eisenhower! Mr. Eisenhower wants to "point up" "steady military gains," albeit he does not really mean military gains; he means, as the preceding paragraph shows, a reorganization of the Department of Defense. He is gratified by the achievements these gains represent, although gains (or achievements) do not *represent*, they *exist*, or else they are not achievements. He tells us in three successive sentences that armaments are purchased at great cost, that our rearmament costs sixty per cent of the Federal budget, and that modern weapons are exceedingly expensive; and, even if repetition is a form of emphasis, the movement of this rhetoric is circular and not forward, as, indeed, the movement of seven succeeding paragraphs, each of one sentence, is also circular.

The reader does no work in Mr. Eisenhower's case. All the work is done for him by the writer. In the Gladstone passage, on the other hand, the reader has to do just enough work to keep him interested in both style and content. "Not yet too late . . . to become competitors for that prize"—somehow that awakens an echo in the mind. "A single leaf of that immortal chaplet of renown"—where does that come from? "The reward of true labour in that case"—the cadence is vaguely familiar. Why is all this somehow more satisfactory than Mr. Eisenhower's prose?

The answer is simplicity itself. Mr. Eisenhower, in a business civilization, talks the language of our chambers of commerce; Gladstone, the product of Eton and Oxford, has be-

[2] *New York Times*, 10 January 1959, p. 6.

hind him the weight of a long cultural heritage. His cadences suggest, though they do not copy, the cadences of Milton's *Areopagitica*. They recall the famous sentence about a fugitive and cloistered virtue that never sallies out and sees her adversary, but slinks out of the race where that immortal garland is to be run for, not without dust and heat. Indeed, Milton's phrase about an old man eloquent comes to mind when one thinks of Gladstone, who has, as I say, the weight of a whole culture behind him, whereas behind Mr. Eisenhower's budget message—and budget messages were Gladstone's specialty—there is no cultural weight whatever, but only a kind of political common sense, a sort of television heartiness, as if the President of the United States were the chairman of a numerous and unruly board of directors not in sympathy with the purposes of the firm. Gladstone, for all his defects, impresses one as a statesman who cares about culture, who is the product of culture, who believes that culture in the Arnoldian sense is in the long run likely to prevail. As I am not interested in Mr. Eisenhower's politics but only in his prose, let me say that the final paragraphs of his message include the statement of a creed; namely, that "we march in the noblest of causes—human freedom" and that we must "make ourselves worthy of America's ideals." But these excellent sentiments, to which everyone will instantly subscribe, do not quite pass the subtle line that separates the commonplace from the memorable.

My point is not that Mr. Eisenhower is a mediocre prose writer—most American presidents lack any distinction of style—or that Gladstone is always elevated, always rich. Here, for example, is a passage by him from a budget debate of 1866 which seems to me to illustrate the pompous sublime and to be probably one of the most unconsciously funny things in the three hundred thousand papers Morley talks about. It concerns pepper.

We propose to remove the duty on pepper. The fate of pepper might well excite the commiseration of any humane man. . . . The present, therefore, appears to be a good occasion when, without exciting feelings of jealousy in the agriculturist or any other class of the community, we can afford to do justice to pepper. The case is a hard one, and for this reason; all the spices and condiments in which the wealthier classes have an exclusive interest have been long ago set free from duty. But pepper is a condiment common to all classes of the community; and though I cannot say whether this is so or not, I am told that it is largely consumed in Ireland.[3]

This is sheer fatuity.

Nevertheless, something decisive has happened to the concept of style in our time as contrasted with the concept of style for the generation of 1830. On the one hand, verse, as represented by Mr. Aiken's poem—and Mr. Aiken is by no means the most opaque of recent poets—has developed a style that minimizes the responsibility of the writer to communicate with the reader. Like abstract painting, if you don't understand the poem, it is just too bad. On the other hand, prose—and the prose of Mr. Eisenhower at least lacks gobbledygook and fairly represents the level of our public prose—accepts no responsibility whatever for maintaining a cultural tradition. Our public prose is shaped by non-literary considerations that revel in such half-truths as that short sentences are better than long sentences, a principle which, if it were true, would rule out the last third of the Gettysburg Address; or that Anglo-Saxon words are better than Latin derivatives, a principle which, if it were true, would ruin the opening paragraph of "The Fall of the House of Usher"; or that informality of approach is better than formal organization, a principle which, if it were true, would lead us to cast aside Lincoln's famous speech at the Cooper Institute in New York in 1860. *Our* notions of prose, in fact, deny that literary tradition has any relevance to modern writing and require the novelist, the statesman, the economist, and the scholar, if they have any culture, to conceal this stain upon their verbal honor. On the

---

[3] *Hansard*, 3rd ser., CLXXXIII (1866), cols. 382–383.

one hand, it is clear, the style of most modern poetry accepts little or no responsibility for public communication; on the other hand, the style of most modern prose accepts little or no responsibility for tradition and culture.

The generation of 1830 did not all write alike. Style with them is personalized and individual. One cannot quite conceive of Oliver Wendell Holmes writing "The Masque of the Red Death," just as one cannot quite conceive of Charles Darwin writing the *Rubaiyát of Omar Khayyám*. But in another sense—in the sense that every great period has its own resonance—these individual styles melt into something great and lasting, something that gives these men, whatever their private griefs, a common appearance of solidity, a sense of strength that may, indeed, deceive us about their inner uncertainties but that seldom deceives us about their skill. You feel instinctively you can put yourself into their hands, whereas you are never quite sure what is going to happen if you put yourself into the hands of a modern poet or a contemporary columnist on public affairs. To say that in the matter of style the elder men do not commonly let you down—despite my paragraph from Gladstone about pepper—is to say that they are in harmony with the resonance of their great age.

What is the central quality of this common style, this resonance? I shall call it a style of responsibility. In every case, even that of Fitzgerald, who is the most fantastic mannerist of the lot, this responsibility is a double responsibility. It looks before and after. It begins with present responsibility to a reader. These men agree with Conrad's preface to *The Nigger of the Narcissus:* "My task which I am trying to achieve is, by the power of the written word, to make you hear, to make you feel—it is, before all to make you *see*. That—and no more, and it is everything." But they are not content with this principle alone, great and central and radical as this duty is for the writer. They have a second great responsibility—a concern for tradition, a concern that the patterns of English speech shall

58

not die out with them, that these inheritances from the spacious days of great Elizabeth and beyond shall be retained and enriched.

To publish is to make public; and the men of 1809, however they might differ in individual manner, did not feel they had discharged their whole obligation until their poetry and their prose had met these two central obligations: the duty of force, of clarity, and of order on the one hand, and the duty of elegance and historicity on the other. Even Darwin, superficially the least aesthetic of the group, a writer who superbly meets the tests of force, clarity, and order, likewise has this sense of elegance, this sense of historicity, evident not only in the judicious and modest estimates of what the writings of others have contributed to *On the Origin of Species,* but evident also in the great concluding portion of his masterpiece: "Thus, from the war of nature, from famine and death, the most exalted object which we are capable of conceiving, namely, the production of the higher animals, directly follows. There is a grandeur in this view of life, with its several powers, having been originally breathed into a few forms or into one; and that, whilst this planet has gone cycling on according to the fixed law of gravity, from so simple a beginning endless forms most beautiful and most wonderful have been, and are being, evolved." A passage of this sort illustrates historicity because, in the first place, it accepts the obligation to live in a tradition of noble prose, the cadences, to my ear, suggesting the movement of Bishop Butler in *The Analogy of Religion, Natural and Revealed;* and in the second place, because the writer is consciously constructing a great architectural work, he is writing no mere *ad hoc* scientific report, he is adding a philosophic volume to the noble line of English empirical thought.

The discharge of this double responsibility seems to me the quintessential part of their literature. The men of 1830 did not always achieve the richness of Burton or of Browne; they seldom or never attained the concise impersonality we admire in Hemingway; they were frequently diffuse, frequently didactic, frequently overconfident that mere rhetoric is a good in itself—witness Poe and Holmes—but their common style is a better style than anything we have, a style usually flexible, frequently sonorous, capable of haunting felicity and a wide range of effects, but above all a style possessed of what I have tried to define as cultural responsibility to the contemporary public and to the obligation of literary tradition—what Samuel Daniel in a noble phrase called "the treasure of our tongue."

Prose and Pictures:
James Fenimore Cooper

An address prepared for the Cooper centennial in Cooperstown, New York, in 1951. Previously published in *Tulane Studies in English,* Vol. III (1952), 133–154.

THE centenary of the death of James Fenimore Cooper occurred in 1951. In September of that year the New York State Historical Association, which has its home in Cooperstown, joined with the Society for Colonial History and the New York Folklore Society in a three-day program examining the significance of the novelist and of his father in the economic, political, and cultural development of the country. So far as I know, this program was the only official recognition of the centennial. Since we in America are mystically impressed by the passing of a hundred years, this neglect of a great American figure is a little remarkable.

I say "great" advisedly, for Cooper was, in succession to Franklin, Washington, and Jefferson, the American who achieved the greatest international repute in his own lifetime. As a writer he influenced the development of fiction from Russia to the United States. He was translated into every European language. He was praised by personages as different as Sir Walter Scott, Balzac, and Charles Sealsfield (Karl Postl). He fixed the image of America for thousands of Europeans, some of them immigrants to the New World. Even today, the leading Cooper scholar in Europe, M. Clavel, as he informed the conference in

Cooperstown, finds it rewarding to have devoted his life to the study of Cooper's works and of their cultural significance.

I do not imply that American scholars have neglected Cooper, or that literary critics have ignored him, or that a few historians have not tried to estimate his worth. But when one compares the critical enthusiasm for Melville with the relative sobriety of scholarly interest in Cooper—in the twenty years preceding the centenary of Cooper's death scholars published 249 articles on Melville, totaling over two thousand pages, but only 67 articles on Cooper, totaling 561 pages—one begins to sense the difference. Either Cooper is not as important to us as he once was, or we have lost the historical perspective necessary to understand his significance.

One of our difficulties is the persistence of the formula that Cooper wrote the Leatherstocking Tales and that these are boys' books. At the Cooperstown meeting, for example, there were displayed the latest editions of books by Cooper and copies of the latest works about him. These last fortunately included Mr. James Grossman's adult and perceptive biography, a book which puts the scholars to shame in one sense because, untroubled by tradition, Mr. Grossman read the novels to see what they mean rather than accept what tradition says they mean. But aside from Mr. Grossman everything else was for juveniles. A biography for children was officially published while the meetings were in session. New editions of *The Deerslayer, The Last of the Mohicans,* and *The Prairie* were displayed, obviously got up for youth. There were seven books in the Comics Classics, transmogrifying seven of Cooper's novels into comic strip art; and if some scholars present took comfort in this odd form of immortality, to others it looked like the end of Cooper as a literary genius. The situation was succinctly put by one scholar, when he said that while it was fun to study Cooper and fun to talk about him, it is apparently no longer fun for adults to read him.

There is a second reason for the neglect of Cooper, and this

62

is found in the influence of Mark Twain's essay, "The Literary Offences of James Fenimore Cooper," a work so destructive as to lead Professor William Charvat to refer to Twain as Cooper's assassin. Readers of the essay naturally infer that a novelist capable of the blunders Mark Twain satirizes is not worth serious perusal. That Cooper, like Scott and like Mark Twain himself, wrote too much and wrote too hastily, so that he fell into absurdities is true, but to insist upon the absurdities and overlook the genius is not quite fair. Indeed, in this very essay Mark Twain falls into absurdities of his own. For instance, he makes merry over Leatherstocking's ability to hit a nail on the head a hundred yards away with a bullet. But the kind of nailhead Mark Twain has in mind is a modern, machine-made nail, whereas the nail Leatherstocking is shooting at in *The Pathfinder,* in the wilderness, in the mid-eighteenth century was the old hand-wrought nail with a head almost as big as a modern American penny.

As for other marvels attributed to woodsmen and Indians, and so irritating Mark Twain that he said the Leatherstocking Tales should have been called the Broken Twig Series, Mr. Yvor Winters, in one of the best essays on Cooper in print, points out that these skills are no more incredible in their time than is our modern ability to guide two racing automobiles past each other on a narrow road, with only a few inches to spare, a feat that both Leatherstocking and Cooper would have found unbelievable. Yet the acquirement of the practised eye, the exquisite muscular control, and the instinctive confidence necessary to this feat is now so common, it is accomplished a thousand times a day. We think nothing of it, just as we expect airplanes to land on runways and guided missiles to fly to their targets. The utmost Cooper allowed himself in the way of mechanical marvel is the figure-head of the Water-Witch in the novel of that name, which occasionally lights up with an unearthly glow, and produces either music or apt quotations from Shakespeare. There are shocking defects

63

in Cooper, but we ought at least to allow him to live in his own time, closer to the frontier than we are. If it be said that Cooper did not, after all, live on the frontier and that he never knew any wild Indians, the retort is obvious: neither do we. But Cooper had at least the advantage of being closer to the facts than we can be.

To have contributed to world mythology is perhaps the highest form of immortality; and since Leatherstocking has long since joined the company of Uncle Tom, Faust, Helen of Troy, Hamlet and Sherlock Holmes, popular instinct may be right in identifying him with his great creation. But the historian is entitled to sounder views; and unless we see the significance of the scope and variety of his productions, we shall not understand his place in cultural history. I begin, therefore, by insisting that Cooper is by no means merely an Indian novelist. Whether he wrote thirty-one or thirty-two romances is a matter of minor dispute—it depends on how one counts —but let us agree on thirty-one. Of these, only eight are books genuinely Indian in theme. There are eleven novels of the sea, five historical novels principally of events on land, six books of social comment, and some social utopias. We can omit some remarkably bad minor fiction, but we must also reckon with five titles historical in character, including biographical works, and about a dozen volumes of social and political comment and controversy, not to speak of an unknown quantity of uncollected matter, and two (incomplete) volumes of letters.[1]

We might even reduce the number of the Leatherstocking novels, in the sense that *The Pioneers* is not strictly a frontier novel, but a combination of autobiography and social history. When Cooper published it in 1823, he was so far unaware of the possibilities in Natty Bumppo and Chingachgook (here called Indian John), that the Indian principally exists to illus-

---

[1] A complete edition is preparing under the editorship of James Beard.

trate a problem in religious conversion and Bumppo is an inharmonious combination of low class comic character and lawless frontiersman. Because we read Cooper, not with our eyes, but with our memories, the convention is fixed that his principal contribution is Indian stories.[2]

II

It may shock the modern reader into attention to list some of Cooper's unique achievements. He was the first novelist of the sea. He was the first effective novelist of the frontier. He was the first historian of the American navy, and still one of the best. He was the first American novelist to conceive of novels in series. He was the first of our writers to make the succession of generations in a single family the theme of fiction, which he did at least three times—for *The Pioneers* is related to *Homeward Bound* and *Home as Found,* as *Afloat and Ashore* is related to *Miles Wallingford,* and as *Satanstoe* and *The Chainbearer* are related to *The Redskins.* He was the first American novelist to make the morbidity of the New England conscience the theme of major fiction, which he did in *Lionel Lincoln* and again in *The Wept of Wish-ton-Wish.* He wrote the first full-dress social utopia in American fiction, in *The Crater,* preceding it by the anti-utopia of *The Monikins.* He was the first American to write the international novel, and the first in fiction to treat the Tories sympathetically, as in *The Spy* and *The Pilot.* He was also the first professional man of letters in American literature, by which I mean that he was the first writer not a newspaper man or a magazinist to produce books commercially, to depend upon income from them, and to standardize the author-publisher-bookseller relationship, as William Charvat has shown. Finally, he was the only American novelist of international stature

---

[2] So fixed, indeed, that in the edition of Cooper on my shelves, a late novel of social comment, *The Redskins,* is brigaded with *The Prairie* and *The Oak Openings,* which are genuine frontier novels!

65

to take Christianity seriously, both as personal motive and as social force.

Cooper was touched by and touched upon more cultural activities of his period than many of his biographers have let us perceive, including the field of fine arts. He went to school in Albany, then the intellectual and cultural center of upper New York, and there he met the sons of the land-holding aristocrats, whose country seats were painted by wandering limners and whose notions of society Cooper was later to echo. He entered Yale, with its important literary and artistic associations. He served on the sea and on Lake Ontario, an officer mingling with other young gentlemen; and he was commissioned midshipman on the Great Lakes about the time that John Trumbull was painting the first of his several views of Niagara Falls. He married the daughter of an aristocratic Westchester family of Tory sympathies, and lived for some years as a country gentleman in Scarsdale. On Long Island Sound and in New York City he was in contact with prominent writers, artists, and professional men, a vivacious participant in the meetings of the Bread-and-Cheese Club. His first book, *Precaution,* was published in 1820, five years before Thomas Cole settled in New York and unconsciously began the history of the Hudson River school of painters, and four years before William G. Wall brought out his influential *Hudson River Portfolio*—echoed, by the way, in Cooper's last published essay, a comparison of American and European scenery written for *The Home Book of the Picturesque* (1852). From 1826 to 1833 he traveled extensively in Europe, at a time when younger painters were going abroad to return as professional artists; and in Europe Cooper was not only in touch with literary persons like Scott, but with painters like Thomas Cole, sculptors like Greenough, French statesmen, leaders of the Polish Revolt of 1830, and British personages like George Canning. After his return to the New World, he again became the landed proprietor. Opponents in the libel suits which made his later years unhappy but which had important consequence in curbing the anarchy of journalism, were worthy of his steel—men of political or journalistic importance like Thurlow Weed and Park Benjamin. When he died, he was praised by Washington Irving, Emerson, Melville, Hawthorne, Longfellow, Parkman, Webster, Bryant, and others of like calibre. In sum, he moved easily among the makers and shapers of our culture; and if I thus dryly catalogue names, it is only to suggest that his writings are a record, direct or indirect, of cultural development and cultural conflict in an early and wonderful period of American growth.

What are some of these cultural elements?

Let me begin with Cooper's interest in the fine arts. He was the patron of Greenough, influential in securing for that sculptor the commission for his statue of Washington, now in the Smithsonian Museum; and whatever one thinks of the statue nowadays, it is historically of first importance in the development of American sculpture. What is more important, Cooper, as Greenough said, "saved me from despair," by ordering from him—the first work of sculpture commissioned by an American from an American artist—a small marble group called the "Chanting Cherubs." When a storm of prudish protest arose in the New World because the cherubs were nude, Cooper defended the "rare merit of the artist" and refused to be shaken in his allegiance, a fact of some consequence when one studies the mores of the 1830's.

Cooper was also interested in architecture, his views on that vexed problem being set forth, among other places, in *The Pioneers, Home as Found,* and *Afloat and Ashore;* and when, as Oliver Larkin puts it, Greek met Goth in this same decade and was overthrown, Cooper sided with the Goths. In *The Pioneers* he had ridiculed the Jones-Doolittle attempt to turn the Templeton manor house into a specimen of the Greek revival; in *Home as Found* he sends the Effingham family up the Hudson, full of scorn for the "vulgar pretension" of the Greek revival country-seats and public buildings they see from their vessel. John Effingham declares:

The malady has affected the whole nation, like the spirit of speculation. We are passing from one extreme to the other, in this as in other things. One such temple well placed in a wood, might be a pleasant object enough; but to see a river lined with them, with children trundling hoops before their doors, beef carried into their kitchens, and smoke issuing, moreover, from those unclassical objects, chimneys, is too much even for a high taste; one might as well live in a fever.

This looks like the comment of a hard-headed realist, and perhaps it is, but when he got to Cooperstown, the novelist, with the aid of S. F. B. Morse, turned his father's home out of the Greek revival into the new and fashionable Gothic style dwelling, which seems scarcely more compatible with hoop-rolling than does the Hellenic temple.

But though both instances illustrate the closeness of Cooper's concern with movements of taste, it is the field of painting which is of particular importance. His connection with leading members of the Hudson River school was close. Thomas Cole and Thomas Doughty he numbered among his friends. Cooper's European sojourn took place at precisely the period when Cole and Morse were also in Europe, and Morse, Greenough, and Cooper were much together in Paris. Cole, he praised for his vast canvases, "The Course of Empire." Cooper interrupted a late novel, *The Sea Lions,* not merely to denounce those who would rob Robert Fulton of the profits of his invention, but also to testify that Morse "communicated to us his ideas on the subject of using the electric spark by way of a telegraph . . . in Paris, and during the winter of 1831–2, and the succeeding spring, a time when we were daily together; and we have," he adds, "a satisfaction in recording this date, that others may prove better claims if they can." A letter of Cooper's exists in which he considers purchasing Washington Allston's picture, "Elijah in the Wilderness," said to be the first accession made by the Boston Museum.

68

The artists reciprocated by choosing subjects from Cooper's novels for their canvases, Thomas Doughty painting scenes from *The Pioneers,* as did that queer genius, John Quidor, Durand and Dunlap each painting episodes from *The Spy,* Cole from *The Last of the Mohicans,* and J. W. Glass from *The Prairie.* Morse painted a landscape viewed from Apple Hill overlooking Otsego Lake and the source of the Susquehanna; and both John Neagle and John Wesley Jarvis did portraits of Cooper.

The relation of landscape painting by the Hudson River school to Cooper's fictional technique and to his view of life is matter of considerable import. Contemporary fiction has long ceased to be panoramic, and contemporary writing overwhelmingly depends upon town values—so much so that when a "nature" book like Joseph Wood Krutch's *The Twelve Seasons* appears, it tacitly assumes that to be in the country is for the city-dweller an anomalous experience which requires explanation and comfort. Even in William Faulkner's Mississippi country, Yocknapatawpha County, events do not always take place in the open air but within, or close to, man-made dwellings or such human creations as the cemetery. Perhaps the last English novelist formally to set the stage of nature for his action was Thomas Hardy, and the impressive description of Egdon Heath in *The Return of the Native* must be virtually the last grand-scale landscape in any novel.

It follows, I suggest, that as man more and more lives in cities, he becomes more and more alienated from the earth and the sky, and, inevitably, also alienated from the possibility of any closer walk with God. For Cooper the city is artificial, the country normal; and he believed that nature can give opportunity for a closer walk with deity. Consequently we find that Cooper's technique and his assumptions are the precise opposite of ours.

Landscape in America, says Oliver Larkin, passed from being a sideshow into being an art, in the decade extending from Francis Guy's exhibition in New York in 1820 to Joshua Shaw's exhibition in Philadelphia in 1830. This decade also brackets Cooper's progress in fiction from *Precaution* to *The Water-Witch*. In *Precaution* landscape is not a problem, for the natural setting does not exist; but in novels like *The Pioneers, The Pilot, The Last of the Mohicans,* and *The Prairie* landscape is central to the book. Now the characteristic formula for landscapes by the founders of the Hudson River school is this: a dark foreground, usually with one or two trees, commonly dead, and tiny figures looking into the picture; theatrical perspective, so that one views as from a height a vast expanse; winding water in the middle distance extending to the plain of the horizon; the highlight of the central scene and on the distant sky; and silvery cloud or vapor shedding sentiment and vagueness over interminable leagues of earth beyond. This combination of the picturesque and the sublime is evident in most of Cole's landscapes, in works like Doughty's "The Raft" and in Asher B. Durand's "Kindred Spirits," wherein Thomas Cole and William Cullen Bryant are portrayed admiring a mountain waterfall (they look *into* the picture), and the tree, not blasted this time, occupies a fourth of the canvas.

Keeping this formula in mind, let us see how Cooper manages to render Lake George, the setting for the tragic events of *The Last of the Mohicans*. Hawkeye and his companions, Duncan Heyward, the two girls, and the two Mohicans, have escaped from their foes long enough to climb a mountain overhanging the lake, and now look on the landscape under the morning sun, their own backs being turned to the light. Here is how Cooper marshals his words:[3]

The mountain on which they stood, elevated, perhaps, a thousand feet in the air, was a high cone that rose a little in advance of that range which stretches for miles along the western shores of the lake, until meeting its sister piles, beyond the water, it ran off toward the Canadas, in confused and broken masses of rock thinly sprinkled

[3] The passages from Cooper's novels are from the Household edition of the *Works,* 32 vols., as reprinted by P. F. Collier and Son, New York.

with evergreens. Immediately at the feet of the party, the southern shore of the Horicon [Lake George] swept in a broad semicircle from mountain to mountain, marking a wild strand, that soon rose into an uneven and somewhat elevated plain. To the north, stretched the limpid, and, as it appeared from that dizzy height, the narrow sheet of the 'holy lake,' indented with numberless bays, embellished by fantastic headlands, and dotted with countless islands. At the distance of a few leagues, the bed of the waters became lost among mountains, or was wrapped in the masses of vapor that came slowly rolling along their bosom, before a light morning air. But a narrow opening between the crests of the hills pointed out the passage by which they found their way still further north, to spread their pure and ample sheets again, before pouring out their tribute into the distant Champlain. To the south stretched the defile, or rather broken plain. . . . For several miles in this direction, the mountains appeared reluctant to yield their dominion, but within reach of the eye they diverged, and finally united into the level and sandy lands, across which we have accompanied our adventurers. . . . Along both ranges of hills, which bounded the opposite sides of the lake and valley, clouds of light vapor were rising in spiral wreaths from the uninhabited woods, looking like the smokes of hidden cottages; or rolled lazily down the declivities, to mingle with the fogs of the lower land. A singular, solitary, snow-white cloud floated above the valley, and marked the spot beneath which lay the silent pool. . . .

I shall not quote the rest of the description, but at the feet of the observers lie the "extensive earthen ramparts and low buildings" of Fort William Henry, seen in specific detail. Is not this uncommonly like a description of a Hudson River school canvas? It is all there except the tree. One can even see the buildings imagined at Hawkeye's feet, if he will but look at Robert Havell's painting of West Point or the town buildings which line the river in Cole's "Oxbow." Cooper's landscape is composed precisely as landscape paintings by his friends are composed,[4] and he found the effect so efficient

---

[4] I am not inferring that the "source" of the description is in painting, or that Cooper "originates" composed landscapes in fiction. Moreover, the influence of Jefferson's description of the confluence of the Potomac and the Shenandoah, in Notes on Virginia, upon American writing, though not studied in detail, has been great. What I am calling attention to is the specific "structuring" of Cooper's description.

that he never abandoned it. He virtually duplicated this view of Fort William Henry, written in 1826, in a view of Fort Ticonderoga in *Satanstoe* in 1845. The Venetian scenes in *The Bravo,* the Swiss scenes in *The Headsman,* the Florida scenes in *Jack Tier* are painted as a painter would render them. The imaginary landscape of *The Crater,* before Woolston turns the island into a garden, has the same qualities of terror and desolation that Washington Allston achieved in his romantic canvases "Elijah" and "The Deluge." I have even fancied that the dream-like evanescence of the crater in that novel owes something to the fantastic nightmare of Cole, "The Titan's Goblet," painted in 1833. Certain it seems that painter and poet influenced each other, and there is a working relation between the landscape painting of the Hudson River men and the descriptive techniques of New York writers like Irving, Cooper, and William Cullen Bryant.

III

This, however, merely characterizes a mode of statement. What of philosophic meaning? Two fundamental ideas interest the earlier members of the Hudson River school: the theme of the grandeur of God working in the universe; and the theme of the decay of empire, or the assumption that nations like men have their childhood, youth, maturity, old age, and death. Thus Thomas Cole's four pictures, "The Voyage of Life," parallel his first vast canvases entitled "The Course of Empire," the history of culture being for him like the history of the individual. A sense of cosmic power and of cosmic melancholy haunts the paintings of Allston and others—even of so cheerful a soul as John Vanderlyn, who compels one to look at Niagara Falls across a dead tree, with a hawk on its remaining ruined branch. Thus also in Asher Durand's "Morning of Life" the distance is filled with luminous light, but in the companion piece, "The Evening of Life," a Greek building has been replaced by a ruined column, a dead tree, and evening melancholy. In short, the school was torn between the desire to proclaim: "The heavens declare the glory of God, and the firmament sheweth His handiwork"; and the necessity of saying: "What is man, that Thou art mindful of him?"

This conflict is echoed in Cooper, so that those who read him simply as an example of romantic primitivism (exemplified by Natty Bumppo) have not read him well. If in *The Prairie* the dying scout repeats his lament in *The Pioneers* that the beauty of the wilderness has been deformed, the lament is for Cooper not merely poetry but philosophy also. In *The Headsman,* laid in Switzerland, much is made of the sublimity of nature, partly for dramatic effect, but partly also because men ought to listen "to the never-wearied promptings of their impulses in the immediate presence of the majesty of the Creator." In *The Deerslayer,* eight years later, the majesty and calm of the natural world are in constant contrast with the tumultuous passions of men—those very men who, according to primitivism, ought to respond to natural influences. To the discrepancy between the harmony of the universe and the crimes and follies of mankind Cooper returned in *The Wing-and-Wing,* wherein, while admiring the natural beauty of the Mediterranean world, he also declared that

it has been the scene of more ruthless violence, and of deeper personal wrongs . . . than any other portion of the globe.

In *The Crater* he shows how human selfishness ruins an earthly paradise. It is, however, in *The Sea Lions,* his penultimate novel, that Cooper is most explicit on the theme of the effect sublime natural phenomena should have on the human spirit. He writes sadly in the preface:

The physical marvels of the universe produce little more reflection than the profoundest moral truths. A million of eyes shall pass over the firmament of a cloudless night, and not a hundred minds shall be filled with a proper sense of the dread Being that created all that

73

is there—not a hundred hearts glow with the adoration that such an appeal to the senses and understanding ought naturally to produce.

Among this hundred, however, is Roswell Gardiner, hero of the tale, whose conversion to trinitarian Christianity follows upon long exposure to the sublimities of Antarctic scenery and a growing sense of dependence upon God.

Like the painters, like some of the poets, and even like some of the politicians, Cooper was enthralled by the cyclical theory of history, whether interpreted as dependence upon divine providence, or as the ruins-of-empire theme made eloquent by Volney. The intellectual center of Cooper's *The Prairie,* whatever climax the plot may have, is clearly to be found in Chapter XXII, with its lengthy interpolated debate between the aged Leatherstocking and Doctor Obed Battius, in whom Cooper satirizes the pretensions of science. On his side, Leatherstocking insists that the ways of the Lord are past finding out, and more than hints at the failure of the United States to fulfill its destiny; and when Battius outlines world history in scientific terms—the decline of Egypt and Arabia, the exhaustion of nature in Africa, the mute testimony of Thebes and Baalbec to forgotten cultures—Leatherstocking glosses the theory in terms highly suggestive of the Hudson River school.

I quote this eloquent passage at some length, regularizing Cooper's haphazard returns to dialect, and combining two or three speeches or parts of speeches into a single discourse that seems to be central to an understanding of the novelist:

I have lived long, as these gray hairs and wrinkled hands will show, even though my tongue should fail in the wisdom of my years. And I have seen much of the folly of man, for his nature is the same, be he born in the wilderness, or be he born in the towns. To my weak judgment it hath ever seemed that his gifts are not equal to his wishes. . . . If his power is not equal to his will, it is because the wisdom of the Lord hath set bounds to his evil workings. . . . The time has been when I have thought it possible to make a companion of a beast. Many are the cubs, and many are the speckled fauns that I have reared with these old hands, until I have even fancied them rational and altered beings—but . . . the bear would bite, and deer would run, notwithstanding my wicked conceit in fancying that I could change a temper that the Lord himself had seen fit to bestow. Now if man is so blinded in his folly as to go on, ages on ages, doing harm chiefly to himself, there is the same reason to think he has wrought his evil here as in the countries you call so old. Look about you, man; where are the multitudes that once peopled these prairies, the kings and the palaces, the riches and the mightinesses of this desert? . . . They are gone. Time has lasted too long for them. For why? Time was made by the Lord, and they were made by man. This very spot of reeds and grass, on which you now sit, may once have been the garden of some mighty king. It is the fate of all things to ripen, and then to decay. The tree blossoms, and bears its fruit, which falls, rots, withers, and even the seed is lost! Go, count the rings of the oak and of the sycamore; they lie in circles, one about another, until the eye is blinded in striving to make out their numbers, and yet a full change of the seasons comes round while the stem is winding one of these little lines about itself, like the buffalo changing his coat, or the buck his horns, and what does it all amount to? There does the noble tree fill its place in the forest, loftier, and grander, and richer, and more difficult to imitate, than any of your pitiful pillars of a thousand years, until the time which the Lord hath given it is full. . . . From that moment its beauty begins to perish. It lies another hundred years, a mouldering log, and then a mound of moss and earth; a sad effigy of a human grave. . . . As if that was not enough to convince man of his ignorance: and as though it were put there in mockery of his conceit, a pine shoots up from the roots of the oak, just as barrenness comes after fertility, or as these wastes have been spread, where a garden may have been created. Tell me not of your worlds that are old! it is blasphemous to set bounds and seasons, in this manner, to works of the Almighty. . . .

Not primitivism, not romanticism, not the influence of the frontier, not even the mere delight of employing his mytho-poetic power fundamentally shapes the fictional world of Cooper, but a great religious vision of life, one comparable to that in the *Kosmos* of Alexander von Humboldt, a vision at once melancholy and sublime!

This theory and this vision, however, concealed a paradox insoluble alike in history and in contemporary society. On the one hand, a Christian deity had framed explicit moral directions for man, directions which had their most practical form in the Episcopalian church, and which man, especially republican man in America, had only to understand and follow in order to be happy in a young nation in a new world. On the other hand, the law of history was as inexorable for Cooper as it was for Henry Adams—infancy, growth, maturity, decay, death. Perhaps the most any nation could do was to prolong for a time the period of its innocency; and the period of American innocency for Cooper was the classical republic, which vanished with the election of Andrew Jackson. Clearly, no nation ought to hasten the process of its own decay. But when Cooper returned to America in 1833, it seemed to him that this, precisely, was what the Americans were doing.

The social revolution was far along. Tenants insulted their landlords and denied the validity of lawful contracts; speculators lorded it over gentlemen; Yankees from New England outsmarted old families in New York; demagogues libeled their betters in what today we would call smear campaigns; shrill-tongued village Fulvias patronized the gentlewomen who employed them; juries convicted from motives of prejudice rather than in the light of impartial justice; and a false notion of religious liberty led to an exaggerated estimate of self and a total forgetfulness of God.

At the end of *The Crater,* a novel in which Cooper devotes a whole chapter to the disastrous results that follow when men pray at each other and not to God, Cooper writes:

Let those who would substitute the voice of the created for that of the Creator; who shout 'the people, the people,' instead of hymning the praises of their God; who vainly imagine that the masses are sufficient for all things, remember their insignificance, and tremble. They are but mites amid millions of others mites, that the goodness of Providence has produced for its own wise ends; their boasted countries, with their vaunted climates and productions, have temporary possession of but small portions of a globe that floats, a point in space, following the course pointed out by an invisible finger, and which will one day be suddenly struck out of its orbit.

Thus he anticipated the pessimism of Mark Twain. An American Ulysses, who in Europe had known

> cities of men,
> And manners, climates, councils, governments,
> Myself not least, but honored of them all,

he returned to an alien land, and like Shakespeare's Ulysses could exclaim:

> O, when degree is shaked,
> Which is the ladder to all high designs,
> The enterprise is sick! How could communities,
> Degrees in schools, and brotherhoods in cities,
> Peaceful commérce from divídable shores,
> The primogenitive and due of birth
> .   .   .   .
> But by degree, stand in authentic place?
> .   .   .   .
> Take but degree away, untune that string,
> .   .   .   .
> Then everything includes itself in power,
> Power into will, will into appetite;
> And appetite, an universal wolf,
> So doubly seconded with will and power,
> Must make, perforce, an universal prey
> And, last, eat up himself.

In *The Bravo,* published in 1831, Cooper had developed the theme that republican forms in Venice could be manipulated for ends of the deepest ingratitude and treachery, and it is curious how, more and more in the novels he wrote in the forties, ingratitude and treachery emerge as primary forces in American life. In *The Wing-and-Wing* and *The Two Admi-*

77

rals treachery is still European—in the latter, indeed, the loyal American youth foils the treacherous British pretender to an estate. But every subsequent novel is laid in America or concerns Americans primarily. In the *Miles Wallingford* series, lack of commercial good faith almost costs the hero his fortune. In the anti-rent novels popular revenge of fancied wrongs couples with ingratitude. In *The Crater* the villain is demagoguery. The motive forces in *The Sea Lions* are greed and treachery. In *The Oak Openings* treachery is barely outreached by Christianity, and in *Wyandotté* and *Jack Tier* Christianity itself is inadequate to protect virtue on earth, the last named book ending in a climax of weird and cold-blooded murder well-nigh unique in American fiction. The final irony lies in that strange and unappreciated study, *The Ways of the Hour,* in which all that is wrong with American murder trials then and now is pitilessly laid bare, but in which the court, the lawyers, and the jury are eventually outwitted by a heroine who proves to be insane. In some sense the force of cynicism can no further go. Why was Cooper in such despair?

Attempts by historians and special students to put a partisan label on him seem to me mistaken. The man who said on one occasion that he had not attended a political meeting in twenty-five years, who refused the usual public dinner upon his return from Europe, who was never a candidate for office, and who accepted appointment as American consul purely as a matter of convenience—such a man can not be taken seriously as a practical politician, even though he was once a political agent for De Witt Clinton. Attempts to force Cooper into the Whig or Democratic party are vitiated by the simple fact that he tried to be what Walter Lippmann tries to be today—a detached, yet sympathetic commentator on the national scene. He could not remain detached, for the reason that his libel suits involved his personal emotions very deeply; but the difficulty of pinning a partisan label on him is the difficulty of making it stick. If he was the agent of De Witt Clinton, he was the agent of a political independent, like himself democratic in emotion and aristocratic in taste. Though Cooper was furiously assailed by Whig editors as an un-American snob, Henry Clay, Secretary of State in the administration of John Quincy Adams, commonly regarded as the beginning of the Whig party, offered Cooper the post of minister to Sweden!

Cooper's notorious libel suits were not focal to his purpose. That purpose, as I read him, even in his despair, was to see that republican institutions should be richly adequate to the functioning of American life. These institutions should not be twisted into an imitation of the Venetian variety of republic government, nor into mere demagoguery and populism. And if at this distance the term "Venetian oligarchy" seems wildly inappropriate to the United States of 1830 and 1840, let us remember that in England Disraeli did not hesitate so to characterize the Whig ministries, and that other thoughtful Americans feared that the Virginia dynasty, the Albany Regency, or the Kitchen Cabinet of Andrew Jackson might develop into a locus of actual political power unknown to the Constitution. As for vulgarity, demagoguery, and the tyranny of the majority over the cultivated few, Cooper was no harsher in his strictures than was Dickens or Mrs. Trollope, but he had the misfortune to be an American taking the unpopular side.

When Cooper published *Precaution,* James Monroe, last of the great line of Virginia presidents, had, for the second time, been elected to the White House; when Cooper returned to the United States thirteen years later, Andrew Jackson was in his second term. Whatever interpretation one puts on the Jacksonian revolution nowadays, Cooper found in it a revolution. The government of the United States had been shaped by a great gentleman, George Washington, who was also a land-holder. Louisiana had been purchased by a second gentleman having a country house. The Missouri Compromise had been arranged by gentlemen North and South in

79

1820—Henry Clay, for example, with his seat at Ashland. The Monroe Doctrine would presently be proclaimed by another Southern gentleman; and when he was succeeded by a Massachusetts gentleman with an estate at Braintree, Cooper joined a group of New York gentlemen to attend the inauguration of John Quincy Adams in 1825. The most successful man for settling inhabitants on new land in central New York was a gentleman, the novelist's father, Judge William Cooper, foully murdered by a dastardly political opponent; and the greatest boon to the Empire State was the creation of a gentleman named De Witt Clinton. A proper republic, it was evident, was the creature of gentlemen less aristocratic than the British gentry and less doctrinaire than the French nobility, but still, landed gentlemen—virtuous modern Romans who, governing their lives by the principle of *noblesse oblige* and who, making *res publica* a primary philosophical concern, would counsel the electorate, tell the voters whom to put in office, and govern the country for the country's good.

Now this was no longer possible. People like Aristabulus Bragg and Steadfast Dodge, pictured in *Home as Found,* or like Jason Newcome, the Yankee money-getter of the anti-rent novels, were running the country; and though, writing from Europe in 1828, Cooper had said:

In no particular, that I can discover, does the situation of an American gentleman differ from that of an English gentleman, except that the former must be content to enjoy his advantages as a concession of the public opinion, and not as a right,

he presently discovered that what could not be asserted as a right could not be extorted as a concession. Consequently, he was characterizing bodies of men as mobs, "proverbially heartless" and inclined to commit injustice without reflection and to vindicate abuses without remorse; and he declared ten years before his death:

There is no question that the government of this great republic was intended to be of well-considered and upright principles, in which certain questions are to be referred periodically to majorities, as the wisest and most natural, as well as the most just, mode of disposing of them.

These questions were, of course, to be propounded by gentlemen. Cooper continues:

Such a government, well administered, and with an accurate observance of its governing principles, would probably be the best that human infirmity will allow to administer; but when the capital mistake of supposing that mere numbers are to control all things, regardless of those great fundamental laws that the state has adopted for its own restraint, it may be questioned if so loose, and capricious, and selfish a system is not in great danger of becoming the very worst scheme of polity that cupidity ever set in motion. . . . This influence of numbers, this dire mistake of the very nature of liberty, by placing men and their passions above those great laws of right which come direct from God himself, is increasing in force, and threatens consequences which may set at naught all the well-devised schemes of the last generation for the security of the state, and the happiness of that very people. . . .

The vanishing race of public-spirited gentlemen primarily concerned for the commonwealth might come from the merchant class, though Cooper regarded commerce with suspicion; but they were, more normally, gentlemen living on land. In an agrarian republic this need not surprise us. The possession of an estate as the proper economic foundation for public life seemed to Cooper so elementary a need that fifteen out of his thirty-one novels turn in greater or less degree upon the acquisition, inheritance, possession, or loss of landed property. He had seen such estates in actuality and had known their owners—men of the generation of Jefferson and Livingston. There was, for example, William Jay, whose country seat he describes with loving care in *Notions of the Americans*. There was his own father. The instinct for property, he held, had been divinely implanted in the human breast. It might, of course, be warped by greed, as in the case of Deacon Pratt in *The Sea Lions,* but the responsibilities of land, the challenge of public life, the guidance of Christian faith would create and support the kind of selfless statesmen who alone could prevent the commonwealth's decay.

This noble brede were now being hounded by adherents of another faith, uncultured and grasping men, who held to Adam Smith's stake-in-society theory, which Cooper parodied in *The Monikins;* men who repeated all the errors of the rapacious French; men incredibly remote from the merchants of the Renaissance; men who corrupted young men as Rupert Hardinge is corrupted in *Afloat and Ashore* and *Miles Wallingford* and who, being worshippers, in William James's phrase, of the bitch-goddess Success, vitiated the republic. Trade, Cooper declared in 1847, meaning by that a spending economy, is "perhaps the most corrupt and corrupting influence in life," second only to politics. He makes Hugh Littlepage lament that the acquisition of money had, by the middle forties, become the sole incentive to exertion in the country; and at the climax of that agrarian idyll, *The Crater,* just before the happiness of Mark and Bridget Woolston is ruined by demagogues, we find Cooper writing:

As the man who lives only to accumulate, is certain to have all his nobler and better feelings blunted by the grasping of cupidity, and to lose sight of the great objects of his existence, so do whole communities degenerate into masses of corruption, venality, and cupidity, when they set up the idol of commerce to worship in lieu of the ever-living God.

Hugh Littlepage is made to say:

Military fame, military rank, even, are unattainable under our system: the arts, letters and science, bring little or no reward; and there being no political rank that a man of refinement would care for, men must live for money, or live altogether for another state of being.

Small wonder that Cooper's later books are an appeal from Mammon to God.

Before one dismisses such passages as mere crotchety prose or as tedious moralizing, let me point out that Cooper, like

Webster, like Clay, like Calhoun, like, for that matter, Emerson, Thoreau, Irving, and Poe, is trying to ascertain by what principles the nation shall live—or, in modern jargon, trying to make democracy work. His dilemma was a dilemma of culture. He was caught between the agrarian republic and the industrial revolution. He thought in terms of republican theory in a period of democratic populism. He wanted to preserve the Jeffersonian values in the era of Jackson. He insisted that every society was ordered in ranks and classes at a time when the populace moved William Henry Harrison out of a plantation house into a log cabin. Amid the conflict of religions of the age, he insisted upon a traditional faith and an understandable church. If his creed of the responsible gentleman went down to defeat, it was nevertheless a belief that republican leaders should be men of culture and responsibility, a recurrent doctrine in the history of this nation, as any commencement ceremony will demonstrate.

The valuable work of Cooper scholarship in the thirties and forties was to demonstrate that the author of the Leatherstocking stories is a social critic of great value. Inevitably, the interest engendered by this demonstration drew attention from other phases of Cooper's art and thought. The French refer to certain sorts of writers as *moralists,* and it is to the moralist in Cooper that investigation can next, I believe, profitably turn. My analysis demonstrates, I trust, some of the ways in which Cooper as a moralist is involved in the aesthetic and philosophic currents of his age.

Oliver Wendell Holmes (1809–1894)

An address delivered at Miami University, Oxford, Ohio, in 1959.

O F THE great figures whose sesquicentennial was celebrated in 1959 none, I suppose, has dwindled more than Holmes. The reasons are many. One is familial. He was the son of his father, the Rev. Abiel Holmes, who was one of the founders of historical scholarship in this country and also a gentleman of humanity and cultivation who, nevertheless, in the words of Holmes' biographer, taught the horrors of Calvinism—a fact of some consequence in the intellectual development of the poet. The doctor's son was, as all the world is aware, Mr. Justice Holmes of the Supreme Court, and it is probable that for every hundred Americans today who know such phrases by him as "clear and present danger" and "the Fourteenth Amendment does not enact Mr. Herbert Spencer's *Social Statics*" only one can recite any stanza of "Old Ironsides." The poet has been overshadowed by the lawyer as the young doctor was overshadowed by the Calvinist historian.

But descent and paternity do not of themselves explain the decline in the fame of Oliver Wendell Holmes. Other worthies born in 1809 were movers and shakers in a way that Holmes was not. Darwin changed the thought of mankind. Lincoln preserved a nation. Tennyson summed up the idealism of a century. Gladstone was a European statesman. Poe influenced the imagination of the world. Even Edward Fitzgerald, in turning Omar Khayyam from Persian into English, con-

84

tributed importantly to comparative literature. Claims of like weight cannot be made for Holmes. As a medical man, though he fought quackery and stood for modernism, he must share his one contribution to research—the contagiousness of puerperal fever—with the Austrian Semmelweis. As a biographer, he wrote lives of Emerson and Motley that are competent but not distinguished, though the Emerson has some interesting things in it. His solitary travel book, *Our Hundred Days in Europe,* is little more than a social diary which could be charged by an unkind critic with sycophancy, were it not that the old gentleman's vanity is innocent. He wrote a handful of memorable poems such as "The Deacon's Masterpiece; or, The Wonderful One-Hoss Shay," "The Last Leaf," and "The Chambered Nautilus," that linger in school anthologies, but Mr. Eliot has trained us to look elsewhere than to eighteenth-century clarity for poetical excellence; and though there are interesting parallels between Holmes and Mr. Ogden Nash, light verse is at best a frail bark on which to embark for eternity.

The doctor's fiction—the famous "medicated novels," *Elsie Venner, The Guardian Angel,* and *A Mortal Antipathy*—has a certain charm, but scarcely counts in the development of the nineteenth-century novel as a work of art. Our author is an excellent essayist: his *Pages from an Old Volume of Life* contains some delightful things, like "The Seasons," which revolves with the revolving New England year as Mr. Joseph Wood Krutch does in his *The Twelve Seasons;* but even this miscellany, excellent in itself, is only a minor triumph. Finally there is the Breakfast Table series, four volumes running from the *Autocrat* of 1857–58 to *Over the Teacups* of 1891–92, unique contributions to American letters, but perhaps no better than Sterne or Thurber or E. B. White, if as good. I think these volumes are quintessential Holmes, but I am under the impression they are read nowadays, if they are read at all, only in college classes, in selections, and under compulsion. They do not leap to the hand as does, say, *The Practical Cogitator* by two later Bostonians. They do not tell us enough about the plight, or, if one prefers, the blight of man.

Holmes shares, moreover, in the contemporary denigration of his group and generation. Doubtless the nineteenth century had too good a conceit of itself, especially in New England; and the late Fred Lewis Pattee was justified in saying of Barrett Wendell's *Literary History of America,* published in 1890, that it should have been entitled *A Literary History of Harvard College, with Some Attention to the Minor Authors.* When Holmes died, there was little doubt in anybody's mind that Lowell was the American Goethe, Bryant the American Wordsworth, Longfellow the American Tennyson, and Whittier the American Burns. Nowadays, when I examine candidates for the Ph.D. who desire to specialize in American literature, I find they know a great deal about Hawthorne, Thoreau, Melville, and Whitman, but very little about the American Goethe, the American Wordsworth, the American Tennyson, and the American Burns. (On Emerson it is usually touch and go.) They can tell me all sorts of things about James's international novels, but when I ask them why there is a bust of Longfellow in Westminister Abbey, they look indignant, as if I had violated the canons of propriety. A transvaluation of values has overcome nineteenth-century authorship, a change that has put down the mighty from their seats and has exalted them of low degree—a line, by the by, that comes from the *Tales of the Wayside Inn.* Concerning Longfellow, Bartlett's *Familiar Quotations* says that "quotations from that author are included as notes so numerous that the editors consider it impracticable to give the numbers of all the pages where they occur." The decline of many New England reputations has gone hand-in-hand with the decline of New England as a major shaping force in American culture, and in this decline Holmes undoubtedly participates.

Is there anything to be said for Holmes? I think there is

86

something to be said, and my thesis is that whereas other figures—Darwin, Gladstone, Tennyson, Poe—were great national or international performers, in Oliver Wendell Holmes we have parochialism raised to a high power of culture, intelligence, and will. Perhaps parochialism is not the right word, but by what other term shall one designate that attachment to a single plot of ground which informs and strengthens the work of Virgil, Dr. Johnson, and White of Selborne? Even the funeral oration of Pericles is parochial in the sense that the speaker affectionately attributes to Athens the universal values of man; nor should we forget that Thoreau, whom we highway Arabs admire without imitating, once said that he had traveled a great deal in Concord.

Holmes can, of course, be convicted of parochialism in the narrow or perjorative sense. Aside from two trips to Europe spaced more than a half a century apart, he never went anywhere, spending all the rest of his life almost literally in or near Boston. Emerson was a space traveler by comparison. As the utmost of Mrs. Primrose's adventurings was to remove from the blue bed to the brown, so Holmes vibrated between Nahant and Beverley Farms, with an occasional daring summer in western Massachusetts. The two foci of his existence were the Saturday Club and the Harvard Medical School. His friends were New Englanders, his novels are New England novels, the boarding house of the Breakfast Table series is a Boston boarding house, and his common vehicle of publication was *The Atlantic Monthly,* which he christened. He was capable of writing Motley, upon moving into a new residence in the eighteen-seventies: "We have really a charming house, and as I turn my eyes to the left from this paper, I seem to look out on all creation, Bunker Hill, and the spires of Cambridge and Mount Auburn . . . ." The identification of all creation with the environs of Harvard College is a not uncommon confusion, but Holmes could go even further as when, in 1869, he told the Massachusetts Historical Society: "We can point to our capital as the port of entry for the New World of the great medical discoveries of two successive centuries, and we can claim for it the triumph over the most dreaded foe that assails the human body," a statement that must have been read with a certain reserve in, let us say, Philadelphia.

If Holmes was thus parochial in space, he was also limited in time. His intellectual universe was conditioned by that special form of late eighteenth-century culture one knows as Boston Federalism, a phase of American values as difficult to define as is transcendentalism. The world of Boston Federalism was a gentlemanly world, republican rather than democratic, a world of nothing too much, a world of which the Latin poet Horace was, so to speak, the American laureate, a world in which the kindly intentions of the cultivated mind were a surrogate for rational purpose in the cosmic plan. Not for these port-wine gentlemen, their features painted by Copley, their incomes originating in the India trade, or banking, or law, or real estate, any vulgar chance of being damned. Paley was their theologian, not Jonathan Edwards. Their taste in metaphysics like their taste in meter was conservative—hence the parallel in Holmes between his verse and his teleology —and they were perpetually troubled because they had to maintain a nice discrimination between a profound hope that reason and the will of God would prevail and their sardonic sense of the littleness, the vanity, and the foolishness of man. They believed in traditional culture, and they believed that to follow a profession was a good thing; but they were unable to condense their sense of civilization into anything sharp and piercing as Emerson did, and their professional labors seldom mounted to *expertise* as, for example, the professional thinking of Willard Gibbs or John Jacob Astor or Samuel F. B. Morse turned these men into experts. The core of Boston Federalism was, so to speak, intelligence without specialization. Boston Federalists were fearful that specialization in any form, whether law, medicine, commerce, literature, or theology, might be a sin against general culture, against general intelligence; and so, in the highly competitive nineteenth century in which they, or at any rate their descendants, were compelled to live, their tradition faded away. In the opening pages of his Emerson, Holmes innocently sketches some leading members of this group, who founded the *Boston Anthology;* and it is characteristic of the limitation of his own outlook, that he found it necessary to spend thirty pages on Emerson's ancestry without deriving from this survey a single salient trait in that great personality. His biography may be described as the kindly attempt of belated Boston Federalism to account for a genius it could not understand. Holmes can make nothing of Emerson's essay on Swedenborg, but he notes with pleasure Emerson's interest in and his characterization of Montaigne, saying with an air of relief: "The writer who draws this portrait must have many of the same characteristics."

Emerson, the ideal spirit, eventually passed beyond the confines of Boston Federalism; Holmes, the mundane spirit, continued its tradition. The mundane spirit is a limited spirit; and Holmes works within its limitations. His collected works contain no instance of passion whether intellectual or emotional. Elsie Venner, his only attempt at sexuality in the novel of that name, though she suffers, suffers in a distant, smothered, and indirect way. His other women are out of *Godey's Lady's Book.* Over some of these genteel wraiths, the Iris's and the Avis's of the Breakfast Table series, he occasionally grows maudlin as only the late eighteenth century could grow maudlin. He has no knowledge of, no interest in, economics, politics, sociology, save as the Civil War roused him to eloquence; and though Boston was changing under his eyes, though he claimed he had bored that ancient city through and through as if it were a cheese, he knows little or nothing of filthy slums, metropolitan degradation, or laissez-faire immorality. Racial snobbery once or twice pained him, and he

89

has an honorable passage and an honorable poem against anti-Semitism, but, in general, American treatment of immigrants, Indians, and slaves drew from him either mild reproof or none. He was neither Wendell Phillips nor William Lloyd Garrison. He knows nothing of Emerson's over-soul, nor of Melville's white whale, nor of Hawthorne's *Scarlet Letter.* It is characteristic that the index to Morse's two-volume biography of Holmes contains no reference to either Hawthorne or Melville and only one to Edgar Allan Poe. As a medical man he must have seen a good deal of suffering and evil, and one kind of evil, to which I shall come, drew from him noble indignation and a life-long campaign; yet in his kindly universe there are no dark Satanic mills, and we are some light years away from the darkness of William Faulkner, the cold cruelty of Robinson Jeffers, the taciturn Prometheanism of Hemingway.

What, then, do we have? We cannot all be giant-like; and what one finds in Oliver Wendell Holmes is a striking example of the free play of lucid and honest intelligence in limited surroundings over a few great problems of life—the relation of God to man, the relation of heredity to responsibility, the relation of truth to tradition. These are important themes which Holmes, a man of eighteeth-century inheritance living and working in the American equivalent of the Victorian world, treated with eloquence, with humor, with sarcasm, with denunciation; and in doing so he freed a great number of his countrymen from fear and ignorance. If Heinrich Heine asked to be remembered as a soldier in the war of humanity for liberation, Oliver Wendell Holmes—and how prim and proper he seems along side the mercurial and fascinating Jew!—enlisted in the same army and fought with some of the same weapons. A distance separates "The One-Hoss Shay" poem from Heine's "Atta Troll," but the distance is not as great as at first it seems. A man who could write as Holmes did of "one more example of the methods of wringing a dry cloth for drops

90

of evidence," or describe homeopathy as "a mingled mass of perverse ingenuity, of tinsel erudition, of imbecile credulity, and of artful misrepresentation, too often mingled in practice, if we may trust the authority of its founder, with heartless and shameless imposition," is not very remote from the savagery or the wit of the German poet.

The bases for Holmes' antagonism to Calvinistic Christianity were early laid. The psychiatrist may trace this antagonism backward, if he will, to the warfare between parent and son, and it is in this connection interesting to note that Holmes says virtually nothing about his father. Or one can find these origins in Holmes' early discovery of the marvels of science. He tells us in an autobiographical fragment: "Ever since I paid ten cents for a peep through the telescope on the Common and saw the transit of Venus, my whole idea of creation has been singularly changed. . . . If I had been looking on [this] planet [from] outside its orbit . . . I should have seen nearly the same sight as that for which I was paying my dime . . . this little globule, no bigger than a marble, the Earth on which I live . . . I never get over the shock, as it were, of my discovery." Astronomy had a life-long fascination for Holmes, as his poem "Wind-Clouds and Star-Drifts" and the figure of the Astronomer in *The Poet at the Breakfast-Table* alike testify; but he drew from the vastness of the universe and the littleness of earth no such pessimistic conclusion about the damned human race as Mark Twain inferred in *The Mysterious Stranger*. I do not find any sure record of his first discovery of Darwinism, but it is everywhere clear that for him evolution was a form of progress that clearly outmoded Jonathan Edwards and all his following.

"The reason is," he wrote, "that the whole system of beliefs which came with the story of the 'fall of man,' the curse of the father of the race conveyed by natural descent to his posterity, the casting of the responsibility of death and all the disorders of creation upon the unfortunate being who found them a part of the arrangements of the universe when he first made his appearance, is gently fading out of enlightened human intelligence, and we are hardly in a condition to realize what a tyranny it once exerted over many of the strongest minds." This Holmes wrote for his centenary essay on Edwards in 1858; to us, who live in the midst of a Calvinist revival of a sort, the doctrine that man is essentially evil is not thus easily to be dismissed.

Pessimism, however, is not necessarily true because it is attractive; and the century that produced the horrors of Buchenwald and the ferocity of modern war has also created Unesco, believes in universal medical care, and has so much faith in humanity as everywhere to demand education. When Holmes asked, through the mouth of the character called Little Boston, in *The Professor at the Breakfast-Table* that religion, which has been Judaized, Romanized, Orientalized, and Anglicanized, should now be Americanized—by which he seems to mean that every man's "soul has a vote in the spiritual community" without being hounded as schismatic or heretical—he was in one sense inviting Protestant Christianity to commit theological suicide, a conclusion that would have shocked him despite his satirical attacks on the ministry. In another sense, he was only expressing, as he thought, the common-sense of the matter in nineteenth-century post-evolutionary terms. His essay on "Mechanism in Thought and Morals" comes as close to metaphysical greatness as anything he could write, and from it I quote this paragraph, which seems to me central:

The hardest and most painful task of the student of to-day is to occidentalize and modernize the Asiatic modes of thought which have come down to us closely wedded to mediaeval interpretations. We are called upon to assert the rights and dignity of our humanity, if it were only that our worship might be worthy the acceptance of a wise and magnanimous Sovereign. Self-abasement is the proper sign of homage to superiors with the Oriental. The Occidental demands self-respect in his inferiors as a condition of accepting their tribute to him as of any value.

In a sense, Holmes comes out where "The Divinity School Address" had come out, but his premise is different and so is his argument. Whether this be a sound interpretation of oriental religions is irrelevant; what is important is Holmes' profound sense of individual integrity. That is why he could write in *The Autocrat:* "Anything that is brutal, cruel, heathenish, that makes life hopeless for the most of mankind and perhaps for entire races,—anything that assumes the necessity of the extermination of instincts which were given to be regulated,—no matter by what name you will call it,—no matter whether a fakir, or a monk, or a deacon believes it,—if received, ought to produce insanity in every well-regulated mind."

The transition from the grandeur of astronomy to the perfection of human anatomy was easy for Holmes, who never dwelt upon the horrors of the dissecting room, but who was capable of comparing the coiled tube of a sweat gland to a fairy's intestine. A typical utterance is the poem indifferently entitled "The Anatomist's Hymn" and "The Living Temple," in which Holmes, with ingenuity as great as that of any seventeenth-century fantast, works the operations of physiology into praise of the Creator. The labor of the heart, for example, is thus described:

> No rest that throbbing slave may ask,
> Forever quivering o'er his task,
> While far and wide a crimson jet
> Leaps forth to fill the woven net
> Which in unnumbered crossing tides
> The flood of burning life divides,
> Then, kindling each decaying part,
> Creeps back to find the throbbing heart.

To such a mind astronomy and geography do not exhaust the glory of God; on the contrary,

> Look in upon thy wondrous frame,—
> Eternal wisdom is the same!

The scientist prays that in old age and death,

> When darkness gathers over all,
> And the last tottering pillars fall,

God will

> Take the poor dust Thy mercy warms,
> And mould it into heavenly forms.

Holmes clung to a belief that the scientist is one who thinks God's thoughts after Him, a theory that rests, so to speak, upon the Federalist culture of Boston, but a theory he could maintain only by silently altering his notions of Deity. "I have a creed," he wrote in *The Autocrat*. "It is told in two words—the first of the Paternoster. And when I say these words I mean them." No doubt. But on the same page we read that "the fluent, self-determining power of human beings is a very strictly limited agency in the universe," which is, of course, the thesis of *Elsie Venner*. If human powers are thus strictly limited, of what importance is the fatherhood of God? Holmes might blast the theological doctrine of "hereditable guilt" as "the doctrine of man's being a blighted abortion, a miserable disappointment to his Creator, and hostile and hateful to him from his birth" and substitute for it an evolutionary meliorism concerning man as "the latest terrestrial manifestation of an ever upward-striving movement of divine power," but he did not perceive, or perceived uneasily, that his argument is as broad as it is long: that, in sum, if the ante-natal moral poisoning of Elsie Venner in the novel is a matter over which she has not the slightest control and for which she has not the slightest moral responsibility, talk about the fatherhood of God is as irrelevant as talk about the guilt of Adam. The plot betrays his bafflement. Having literally done no harm to anybody, Elsie dies, as it were, of the fifth act. Holmes' dilemma was the dilemma of his century.

He tried to solve it as his contemporary Tennyson tried to solve it (and as we try to solve it), by simple affirmation:

> O yet we trust that somehow good
> Will be the final goal of ill

Defects of nature, sins of will,
And all the evil in the blood.

Holmes might write as he did in "Currents and Counter-Currents in Medical Science" that "the more positive knowledge we gain, the more we incline to question all that has been received without absolute proof"; but, child of the eighteenth century, he was not going to question the benevolence of deity. The human will might be in large measure determined by ante-natal and environmental circumstance, but it was not wholly so determined; the human machine might be a wonderful mechanism, but it was not merely a mechanism; and after biology, physiology, physics, chemistry, and materia medica had claimed their own, there was still a mysterious residue, a force in nature even if it was nothing more than the *vis medicatrix naturae* that was evidence of divinity gradually revealed. Here are characteristic utterances from his lecture called "Border Lines of Knowledge in Some Provinces of Medical Science," delivered two years after the publication of the *Origin of Species:*

The problem of force meets us everywhere, and I prefer to encounter it in the world of physical phenomena before reaching that of living actions. It is only the name for the incomprehensible cause of certain changes known to our consciousness, and assumed to be outside of it. For me it is the Deity Himself in action. . . . Our reverence becomes more worthy, or, if you will, less unworthy of its Infinite Object in proportion as our intelligence is lifted and expanded to a higher and broader understanding of the Divine method of action. [Scientific discoveries] all lead us up to the inspiration of the Almighty which gives understanding to the world's great teachers. To fear science or knowledge, lest it disturb our old beliefs, is to fear the influx of the Divine wisdom into the souls of our fellow-men; for what is science but the piece-meal *revelation*—uncovering—of the plan of creation, by the agency of those chosen prophets of nature whom God has illuminated from the central light of truth for that single purpose?

This is charming and perhaps it is true, but the picture of men like Dr. Jackson, Pasteur, and Sir William Osler being

95

in the line of succession to Moses, Isaiah, and Jesus Christ completely shifts the ground of Holmes' original argument. It also makes it difficult to understand why the good doctor, with this mystique of science in his blood, fell foul of Emerson's over-soul as mere talk about the infinite in terms borrowed from the finite. Practical-minded Federal Boston takes over, however, in Holmes' inquiry concerning the lesser transcendentalists: "What forlorn hope have you led? What immortal book have you written? What great discovery have you made? What heroic task of any kind have you performed?"

I find, however, on re-reading Holmes, that his interest for moderns lies less in his jejune theory that divine guidance (or revelation) in scientific inquiry somehow antiquates Jonathan Edwards than in his anticipations, often startling, of some of the doctrines of psychology. His medicated fiction has been considered by some historians to anticipate the theories of Freud and Jung. Dr. Clarence P. Oberndorf, for example, has published a study called *The Psychiatric Novels of Oliver Wendell Holmes*. In each of the three tales we are presented with a child left motherless at an early age and subjected to some sort of austere and unsympathetic force; in each we deal with an obsession developed in childhood; in each there is a sympathetic physician who watches over the central personage; and in each the narrative carries hero or heroine to cure or to destruction. The first and third stories—*Elsie Venner* and *A Mortal Antipathy*—focus upon infantile shock. *The Guardian Angel* vaguely foreshadows the collective unconscious of Jung and deals with the problem of multiple personality. All this is true enough, but we do not have to go to Europe to ascertain the originality of Holmes. We have only to turn to the masterpiece of another son of Harvard, *The Principles of Psychology*, of William James, published in 1890, four years before the death of Holmes and one year before the appearance of *Over the Teacups* in volume form. One of the central doctrines in James appears in the great chapter

96

on the nature of consciousness. In *Over the Teacups,* one finds Holmes' tribute to James for his "full exposition of the doctrine of plural personality."

The culture of Federalist Boston, for all its worldliness and its urbanity, was an inward-looking, a brooding consciousness, concerned for the attributes of personality. If I were called upon to define the most "modern" theme in the twelve volumes of Holmes' complete works, I think I should select the nature of consciousness in its relation to personality. The entire Breakfast Table series, from *The Autocrat* to *Over the Teacups,* is, in a sense, nothing more than the expression of the author's multifaceted personality—autocrat, professor, poet, sage. The novels are quasi-laboratory reports on personality problems. The two biographies are patient attempts at the analysis of striking personalities, and the remaining volumes (including the poetry) contain many passages concerning the development of personality, the relation of personality and freedom, and the meaning of consciousness.

His work as an anatomist possibly focussed Holmes' attention upon the leading role heredity plays in psychic life. When Harriet Beecher Stowe inquired what he really meant in *Elsie Venner,* he wrote that he wanted to "stir up" the question of automatic agency in relation to self-determination and that he used the rattlesnake to dramatize the truth that personality may be shaped by an "unconscious, intuitive tendency, dating from a powerful ante-natal influence which modifies the whole organization." He thought no malformed character wholly shapes (or mis-shapes) itself, as this trenchant passage from *The Poet at the Breakfast-Table* makes clear: "People hold up their hands at a moral monster as if there was no reason for his existence but his own choice . . . ; study . . . will teach you that you do not get such a malformed character . . . without a long chain of causes to account for it; and, if you only knew these causes, you would know perfectly well what to expect." Hang him, if it is for the good of society, he continued, but "recognize the fact that what you hate in him is chiefly misfortune, and that if you had been born with his villainous low forehead and poisoned instincts . . . you would not have been sitting there in your gold-bowed spectacles . . . passing judgment on the peccadilloes of your fellow creatures." Waiving the question whether the actions of a character like Popeye in Faulkner's *Sanctuary* are peccadilloes, one notes to what an astonishing degree Holmes' doctrine anticipates the assumptions of many modern novelists.

If many components of personality are for him inheritances, Holmes was equally impressed by the influence of environment in shaping consciousness, as the famous passages about the Brahmin caste and about quality and equality exist to prove. The Americans, he wrote, are touchy about social distinctions, but it is as impossible to avoid them as to avoid recognizing the facts of natural history. Environment shapes personality. Changes in our manner of existence, he wrote in 1861, imply that "we have experienced some very profound impression which will sooner or later betray itself in permanent effects on the minds and bodies of many among us"; and he noted the increase of what we would call psychosomatic symptoms in New England during the first months of the Civil War. His explanation might have been written by William James: "The same trains of thought go tramping round in one circle through the brain, like the supernumeraries that make up the grand army of a stage-show. Now, if a thought goes round through the brain a thousand times in a day, it will have worn as deep a track as one which has passed through it once a week for twenty years."

In such passages Holmes is talking about matters external to consciousness; what of the operations of consciousness itself? The more Holmes studied the matter, the more unpredictable, the more complicated he found the matter to be. He compares the operations of men's minds to the varied moves in chess; he returns again and again to the idea that when two persons converse, multiple personalities may be engaged in talking—John and Thomas as they are each to himself, John and Thomas as they are to each other, John and Thomas as they are in the eyes of God. He was more and more fascinated by both the unconscious operations of the mind and by what we, following James and others, call the stream of consciousness. The Poet says in *The Poet at the Breakfast-Table:* "Some kinds of thoughts breed in the dark of one's mind like the blind fishes in the Mammoth Cave. We can't see them and they can't see us; but sooner or later the daylight gets in and we find that some cold, fishy little negative has been spawning over our beliefs, and the brood of blind questions it has given birth to are burrowing round and under and butting their blunt noses against the pillars of faith . . . some of our old beliefs are dying out every year, and others feed on them and grow fat." "My thoughts," observes the Professor, "flow in layers, or strata, at least three deep. I follow a slow person's talk, and keep a perfectly clear under-current of my own beneath it. Under both runs obscurely a consciousness belonging to a third train of reflections, independent of the two others." And the same personage sagely observes: "We shall probably never have the least idea of the enormous number of impressions which pass through our consciousness, until in some future life we see the photographic record of our thoughts and the stereoscopic picture of our actions. There go more pieces to make up a conscious life or a living body than you think for."

A long autobiographical passage in the volume is a proleptic example of what James was to call the blooming, buzzing confusion of conscious life—Holmes talking about a "keyboard of nerve-pulps, not as yet tanned or ossified, to the finger-touch of all outward agencies . . . the filmy threads of this web of life in which we insects buzz a while." The creative consciousness of the poet was, he thought, of this nature; and there is poignancy in reading the many passages in which Holmes, who longed for poetical fame more than he longed for anything else, broods over the psychology of art, alternating between the romantic concept of God-given genius and the late eighteenth-century idea of decorum, craftsmanship, and imitation.

In a psychic universe of this sort, the idea of conscious control, of choice, of freedom of the will more and more diminished. A footnote to the standard edition of *The Professor at the Breakfast-Table* gives us Holmes' final estimate:

The more I have observed and reflected, the more limited seems to me the field of action of the human will. Every act of choice involves a special relation between the *ego* and the conditions before it. But no man knows what forces are at work in the determination of his *ego*. The bias which decides his choice between two or more motives may come from some unsuspected ancestral source, of which he knows nothing at all. He is automatic in virtue of that hidden feeling that he is self-determining.

This, oddly enough, approaches the very doctrine of Jonathan Edwards that he denounced, but Holmes cannot shake off his cultural inheritance, he cannot think of men as machines walking, he had to keep God and vitalism in the universe, he had to retain an ideal end for science. And the same essay which proclaims that "the more we study the will in the way of analysis, the more strictly does it appear to be determined by the infinitely varied conditions of the individual," also declares that men are free and responsible agents in proportion as they feel themselves to be free! Here is the passage:

In spite of the strongest-motive necessitarian doctrine, we do certainly have a feeling, amounting to a working belief, that we are free to choose before we have made our choice. We have a sense of difficulty overcome by effort in many acts of choice. We have a feeling in retrospect, amounting to a practical belief, that we could have left undone the things that we have done and that we could have done the things that we ought to have done and did not do, and we accuse or else excuse ourselves accordingly.

Doubtless a logician can reconcile these statements with Holmes' belief that the laws of human nature are generalizations of the fact that every organ obeys its proper stimulus, but the lay mind finds a certain difficulty in the task.

I spoke earlier of Holmes as exhibiting parochialism raised to a high power of culture, intelligence, and will. His firm rootage in the traditions of Boston prevented his ever approximating the vagaries of a genius like Strindberg or D. H. Lawrence, but at the same time it limited him. In *The Autocrat* he says that "the fluent, self-determining power of human beings is a very strictly limited agency in the universe," and he defined the chief planes of its limitation as organization, education, and condition. The same thing is true of Holmes in actuality. The logic of his thinking about the limits of responsibility should have led him to endorse nineteenth-century naturalism, but he read the death-bed scene in *Madame Bovary* with horror and charged the naturalists with being obsessed by filth. His explorations of the stream of consciousness should have led him in the direction of the association of ideas as a mode of poetry; his culture kept him within the confines of the late Augustan poetic manner modified by Regency wit. His medical doctrine was essentially democratic, inasmuch as all men are equally imperfect, equally the products of heredity; his social training kept him to an elegant republicanism. He hovered on the edge of philosophical determinism, but his urbanity rebuked his pessimism, and, child of a hopeful era, he thought that God and science would ever move from more to more, so that his most famous serious poem could conclude with a promise of perfect freedom:

> Build thee more stately mansions, O my soul,
>   As the swift seasons roll!
>   Leave thy low-vaulted past!
> Let each new temple, nobler than the last,
>   Shut thee from heaven with a dome more vast,
>   Till thou at length are free,
>   Leaving thine outgrown shell by life's unresting sea!

Here is the incorrigible optimism of much American thought, and I think it significant that Holmes, whose biography of Emerson is commonly said to be inadequate because of the lack of sympathetic understanding between Cambridge manners and Concord dreams, comes in fact thus to parallel the poetic epigraph for Emerson's *Nature:*

> A subtle chain of countless rings
> The next unto the farthest brings;
> The eye reads omens where it goes,
> And speaks all languages the rose;
> And, striving to be man, the worm
> Mounts through all the spires of form.

Holmes found Emerson's book a poetic anticipation of evolution—"evolution of the best and elimination of the worst as the law of being," he said. Perhaps the unity of New England thought in the nineteenth century was greater than we had supposed.

Arnold, Aristocracy, and America

Previously published in *American Historical Review,* Vol. XLIX
(April 1944), 393–409. Since this essay was written, further information on Arnold's American tour has appeared, but I find little
to alter my interpretation.

O N Monday morning, October 15, 1883, the Cunarder
Servia slowly worked its way to the dock in New York whereon
Andrew Carnegie, then forty-eight years old, awaited with
his secretary the disembarking of three English guests. These
were Mr. and Mrs. Matthew Arnold and their daughter, Lucy.
Arnold was sixty-one years old, "tall, well-formed, with an
air of high breeding and refinement," though his face was "not
sicklied o'er with the pale cast of thought," according to the
reporter who "covered" his first American lecture. A Chicago paper was less generous: "He has harsh features, su-
percilious manners, parts his hair down the middle, wears a
single eyeglass and ill-fitting clothes."[1] The aging Victorian had
been transformed by success from the sprightly worldling who
wrote letters full of banter to Arthur Hugh Clough into the

[1] Accounts of Arnold's American tour have been published many times.
See, *inter alia,* E. P. Lawrence, "An Apostle's Progress: Matthew Arnold in
America," *Philological Quarterly,* X (Jan. 1931), 62–79; James Dow McCallum, "The Apostle of Culture Meets America," *New England Quarterly,*
II (July 1929), 357–81; James Bentley Orrick, "Matthew Arnold and
America," *London Mercury,* X (Aug. 1929), 389–97; Lionel Trilling, *Matthew Arnold* (New York, 1939), pp. 392 ff. Arnold's own reminiscences
may be read in his *Civilization in the United States: First and Last Impressions of America* (Boston, 1888). This is a compilation of four essays
printed in various periodicals in the eighties.

pontifical spokesman of a cult. A series of one hundred speaking engagements awaited him, apparently arranged by Richard D'Oyley Carte, of Savoy opera fame, and Major James Burton Pond, the most notable manager of lecturing "talent" in the United States. The essayist looked forward with only a momentary qualm to the ordeal of addressing audiences in a country to which, as he had candidly written a friend, he hated to go.[2] He had been lecturing in England with considerable success. There had been a "crowded audience" at Cambridge in the summer of 1882 for one of the lectures he proposed to repeat in the United States; 1,200 had heard him at Liverpool the following October; and if, when he spoke before the Wordsworth Society at Westminster in the spring of 1883, the half-filled hall and listless audience reminded him of the grave, this was exceptional, some functionary had "muddled things." In his own country even "the railway porters and guides have read my books," he had been told. He had brought along plenty of letters of introduction, for he had learned that James Russell Lowell, the American minister in London, "only knows . . . Boston and Cambridge," so that Lowell's advice on social points could not "be followed for America generally." He had also brought two lectures; and the mere fact that one had already been published and the other already delivered seemed to him inconsequential, since to the one entitled "Literature and Science" he had prefixed "a new introduction, to fit it for America." A third lecture (on Emerson) was unwritten, but "a Mr. Clarence King, a charming man, tells me his mother has a villa at Newport, where I can go and be entirely free for a week, and enjoy the last of the autumn while . . . composing my Emerson."

Without delay about the baggage the Arnolds were borne off to the Windsor Hotel, where Carnegie lived with his

---

[2] Much of the material in this section is gleaned from *Letters of Matthew Arnold, 1848–1888,* collected and arranged by George W. E. Russell (2 vols., New York and London, 1895), II, 233 ff.

mother, in rooms papered with tartan.³ A suite awaited them, over the doors of which floral pieces had been affixed, each inscribed with a title from one of Arnold's books—"Literature and Dogma," said one; "Culture and Anarchy," read another. "In a few minutes," as Carnegie's biographer innocently remarks, "the Arnold family found themselves completely at home." Arnold and Carnegie had first met in London in June at a dinner given by Yates Thompson, editor of the *Pall Mall Gazette*, when the ironmaster had urged the apostle of culture to cross the seas.

Although Arnold had never set foot in the United States, he had several times discussed American culture, most recently in "A Word about America," published in the *Nineteenth Century* for May, 1882.⁴ Writing Sir Mountstuart Grant Duff in July, he had hinted that he really knew very little about life in the republic. "One had," he said, "to trust a great deal to one's 'flair,' but I think my 'flair' served me here pretty well." He had learned that Henry James (who by 1882 was almost as ignorant of America as Arnold was), on being requested to confute the essay, confessed his inability to do so, "it was so true." A Boston paper had furnished Arnold his cue:

In towns whose names Mr. Arnold never heard, and never will hear, there will be found almost invariably a group of people of good taste, good manners, good education and of self-respect, peers of any people in the world. Such people read the best books, they interpret the best music, they are interested in themes world-wide, and they meet each other with that mutual courtesy and that self-respect which belong to men and women who are sure of their footing.

But if this was broad-minded in Boston, it was too inclusive for Arnold. That such persons might exist the essayist did not deny, but that they existed in sufficient numbers to leaven

³ I follow in the main the account by Burton J. Hendrick, *Life of Andrew Carnegie* (2 vols., New York, 1932), I, 243 ff.
⁴ Collected in *Civilization in the United States*, pp. 69–108.

the American lump seemed to him on the whole improbable. England, he reiterated, "distributes itself" into Barbarians, Philistines, and Populace (or, less anagogically, an aristocracy, a middle class, and a proletariat), and America was "just ourselves; with the Barbarians quite left out, and the Populace nearly." (Arnold's ignorance of the labor movement and of American Populism then and always was profound.) And the American middle class, or rather the whole American nation, which was middle class, though it possessed such virtues as industriousness and religiosity, was, he firmly repeated, without culture, that is, without that "type of civilization combining all those powers which go to the building up of a truly human life—the power of intellect and knowledge, and power of beauty, the power of social life and manners, as well as the great power of conduct and religion, and the indispensable power of expansion"—Arnoldese for liberty and equality.[5] Proof of the essential vulgarity of the Americans lay ready at hand—the observations of James Russell Lowell; the uncultivated humor of Mark Twain, whom Arnold strangely compared to Quinion, an obscure character in the second chapter of *David Copperfield;* the description by a Miss Bird of a fearsome family of Reformed Presbyterians living in Denver,[6] whose Sunday was "a dreadful day." Though this last example came from the fringes of civilization, "this hideousness,

---

[5] This definition of civilization is repeated in substance from the lecture on "Equality," which Arnold delivered before the Royal Institute in 1878 and in which he denied the existence of natural rights. "The natural right to have work found for one to do, the natural right to have food found for one to eat—rights sometimes so confidently and so indignantly asserted—seem to me quite baseless." The same address declares a little later: "Property is created and maintained by law. . . . Legal society creates, for the common good, the right of property; and for the common good that right is by legal society limitable. That property should exist, and that it should be held with a sense of security and with a power of disposal, may be taken . . . as a settled matter of expediency." Consult *Mixed Essays,* "Equality" (New York, 1879).

[6] Part of the Arnold legend is the remark of the bishop of Rochester that he feared Denver was not ripe for Mr. Arnold. *Letters,* II, 298.

this *ennui,*" was testimony to the presence and power of "middle-class misgrowths" in the United States he had never seen. Possibly republicans were better off without a royal family and a gentleman class, but were not the defects of American life ineradicable so long as the Americans remained what Lowell had called them, "the most common-schooled and the least cultivated people in the world"? "A higher, larger cultivation, a finer lucidity" were what they needed. Though "an institution like Harvard is probably all one could desire," nothing short of a revolution in secondary education, a turning away from vocational training toward "a serious programme" would suffice to cure New World Philistinism. That the possible perfection of Harvard was not the standard by which to measure the American popular high school, or that the provincialism of that standard might have some connection with Lowell's inability to prognosticate social conduct beyond the Hudson—these were inferences beyond the capacity of a writer who was simply following his flair.

On October 27 there was a reception in the octagonal room of the hotel, Carnegie proudly reporting to John Morley that it "combined more distinguished people than ever before assembled at one time in America." Arnold found it "magnificent" and later (in 1888) referred to Carnegie as "one of the most hospitable and generous of men," author of *Triumphant Democracy,* "a most splendid picture of American progress."[7] He affably shook hands with the hotel steward who had ar-

---

[7] *Civilization in the United States,* pp. 185–86. Arnold here performs a neat trick of legerdemain. "Religious people," said Carnegie's book, insisted "too much on mere material progress"—Arnold's complaint against American life—and "a friendly clergyman in Massachusetts" put into Arnold's hands a volume called *Our Country* as "a good antidote." Arnold thereupon drops the point that Carnegie's book is "too materialistic" to denounce the "entire failure" of the author of *Our Country* to avoid "self-deception." It is interesting to note that Chapter XIII of *Our Country* (by the Reverend Josiah Strong, published through the American Home Missionary Society in 1885) is a glorification of Anglo-Saxon supremacy on evolutionary lines—precisely Arnold's own doctrine.

ranged the flowers, and he admired the way "people, far lower down than us, live with something of the life and enjoyment of the cultivated classes." If newspapermen annoyed him from morning till night, even they, he wrote home, "are better than you would suppose, many of them English adventurers with a history." He had been given the *entrée* at the St. Nicholas Club, the Union Club, the Century Club, and the Knickerbocker Club, the last being "the smart club *par excellence*" in "a beautiful house, splendidly and luxuriantly furnished." He had dined with "some rich people called Shepard. She was a Miss Vanderbilt," and Vanderbilt "is said to be the richest man living, and the house was as splendid as the house of the Rothschilds." Lord Coleridge had also been a dinner guest, "most affectionate," and "his extraordinary eulogy of me" (in a speech delivered October 25) was "freely used as an advertisement for my lectures and books." Amid the flattering attention of the eminent, the dinners of the rich, the life of the exclusive clubs, and the awe of German barbers, he learned without astonishment that 1,250 seats in Chickering Hall had been sold for his first lecture and that people had even paid to stand.

The ensuing catastrophe is famous in the annals of the American lyceum, the classic description being that of Major Pond:[8]

Chauncey M. Depew introduced the speaker. I was looking after the business in the front of the house. There was not a seat to be had excepting a few held by speculators on the sidewalk. As Mr. Depew and Matthew Arnold appeared before the audience, somebody told me that General and Mrs. Grant had just arrived and had seats in the gallery, but some other people were occupying them. I immediately got a policeman, and working through the standing crowd, found that they were the last two seats on the aisles in the gallery.

[8] James Burton Pond, *Eccentricities of Genius* (New York [1900]), pp. 323–24. Other accounts vary in detail, but because of his professional interest in the performance Major Pond should be trustworthy, despite his obvious dislike of Arnold.

We had no difficulty in getting the occupants to vacate as soon as they discovered who held the tickets. We had just heard the last few sentences of Mr. Depew's introduction when Matthew Arnold stepped forward, opened out his manuscript, laid it on the desk, and his lips began to move. After a few minutes General Grant said to Mrs. Grant, "Well, wife, we have paid to see the British lion; we cannot hear him roar, so we had better go home." They left the hall. A few minutes later there was a stream of people leaving the place. All those standing went away early. Later on, the others who could not endure the silence moved away as quietly as they could.

"There is," Arnold wrote his daughter in England, "a good deal to be learned as to the management of the voice, and I have set myself to learn it, though I am old to begin." When he returned to the hotel with the Carnegies, he inquired eagerly: "Well, what have you all to say? Tell me! Will I do as a lecturer?" Carnegie advised elocution lessons, but his mother displayed deeper insight. An Oxford accent had not prevented her from understanding the substance of the address. "Too meeneesterial, Mr. Arnold, too meeneesterial," was her dry comment.[9]

<h2 style="text-align:center">II</h2>

The lecture which the fashionable audience could not hear was, in the words of Arnold's most penetrating biographer,[10] "a curious performance." Entitled "Numbers," and made over from its original form for American consumption,[11] it is as

---

[9] Arnold characteristically consoled himself for this remark by recalling a fulsome compliment from somebody else. "How very right you were," he wrote Mrs. Forster in 1884, "about what you called my too 'solemn' and poor Mr[s]. Carnegie my 'ministerial' manner in speaking. Since I have spoken so much, I have perceived that it is my great defect, inasmuch as it strikes every one. Harper's Magazine goes so far as to say that just because I am irresistibly agreeable to read, I ought never to speak." *Unpublished Letters of Matthew Arnold,* ed. Arnold Whitridge (New Haven, 1923), pp. 53–54.

[10] Trilling, p. 399.

[11] So, at least, I interpret Arnold's ambiguous statement: "I have nearly broken my heart over my first discourse, but I think it will do. It is for

pretty a little piece of antidemocratic propaganda as one can possibly find, even today. In this lecture the audience was suavely informed that the majority is always bad and usually wrong; that a popular state can survive only if it has in it a saving remnant to guide and govern it; that the remnant must know righteousness when they see it; and that the most moral people in the world are the people of Germanic stock—that is, the English. Arnold proves this remarkable fact in two ways. Modern France, he roundly says, is given over to the worship of the goddess Lubricity, whereas the English, including the English in America, are—saving a few faults, such as lack of amiability—the most serious, the most righteous, the most moral people the world has ever seen:

You are fifty millions mainly sprung, as we in England are mainly sprung, from that German stock which has faults indeed,—faults which have diminished the extent of its influence, diminished its power of attraction and the interest of its history. . . . Yet of the German stock it is, I think, true, as my father said more than fifty years ago, that it has been a stock "of the most moral races of men that the world has yet seen, with the soundest laws, the least violent passions, the fairest domestic and civil virtues." You come, therefore, of about the best parentage which a modern nation can have. Then you have had, as we in England have also had, but more entirely than we and more exclusively, the Puritan discipline. Certainly I am not blind to the faults of that discipline. Certainly I do not wish it to remain in possession of the field for ever, or too long. But as a stage and a discipline, and as a means for enabling that poor inattentive and immoral creature, man, to love and appropriate and make part of his being divine ideas, on which he could not otherwise have laid or kept hold, the discipline of Puritanism has been invaluable; and the more I read history, the more I see of mankind, the more I recognize its value. Well, then, you are not merely a multitude of fifty millions; you are fifty millions sprung from this excellent Ger-

New York, and I have now got it in print, and nearly in the exact form in which I hope to give it" (to Mrs. Forster, Oct. 5, 1883, *Letters,* II, 253). I reprint in the text, with slight changes, a portion of my address "American Literature and the Melting Pot," *Southwest Review,* XXVI (Spring 1941), 329–46.

manic stock, having passed through this excellent Puritan discipline, and set in this enviable and unbounded country. Even supposing, therefore, that by the necessity of things your majority must in the present stage of the world probably be unsound, what a remnant, I say,—what an incomparable, all-transforming remnant,—you may fairly hope with your numbers, if things go happily, to have!

No one seems to have challenged the remarkable arithmetic whereby a national population of fifty millions was at once a "saving remnant" sprung from "excellent Germanic stock" and "excellent Puritan discipline" and also a vicious majority lacking "persistence" and wanting proper attention to "whatsoever things are *elevated,*" so that "the failure to mind whatsoever things are elevated must impair with an inexorable fatality the life of a nation" until "the life of even these great United States must inevitably suffer and be impaired more and more, until it perish." No one apparently took the trouble to point out that half of the fifty millions were "immigrants,"[12] most of whom were not of English descent. No one seems to have inquired how, if culture has to do with the best that has been said and thought in the world, culture for Arnold and his audience was somehow left in the exclusive charge of the Anglo-Saxons. For clearly culture could not be left in charge of the Latin peoples, the chief of whom, according to Arnold, was given over to the worship of the goddess Lubricity; nor could culture be put in charge of the Catholic peoples, since, in Arnold's opinion, the discipline of Puritanism is invaluable. Consequently it was to be left in charge of the most moral race of men that the world had yet seen, with the soundest laws, the least violent passions, and the fairest domestic and civil virtues. And by some odd circumstance the representatives of the saving remnant who left sufficient impression upon the lecturer to be recorded in his letters were usually the rich, the prominent, or the well-born.

[12] By 1890, out of a population of 55,000,000 about 24,500,000 were "immigrants."

General Grant had not merely been present at Carnegie's reception, he had called later at the *Tribune* office to thank that paper for the good report of the main points of the inaudible lecture; and to General Grant, Arnold devoted a double essay in *Murray's Magazine* for January–February, 1887, designed to show that Grant revealed "a good deal of the character and qualities which we so justly respect in the Duke of Wellington." From New York Arnold went to Mr. Charles Butler at Fox Meadow, and "from him we went to the Delanos, 90 miles up the Hudson. She was a Miss Astor, and it was like staying with the Rothschilds." In Boston he was admitted to the St. Botolph and Somerset clubs, he was introduced by Oliver Wendell Holmes, he lunched with Whittier, he dined with Charles Eliot Norton, Mrs. Fields, the two daughters of Rufus Choate, Phillips Brooks, "some people called Page, friends of the Wordsworths, who have a fine house in Boston," and with various other Anglo-Saxon worthies. Hospitality in the rest of New England was likewise in the hands of the wealthy or of the right people. At Hartford he stayed with "a nice old couple called Clark"—the richest merchant in "the richest town in New England." At Newport Commodore Vanderbilt put a launch at Arnold's disposal. At Taunton he was a guest at the house "of a Mr. Sanford, who has been Speaker of the State Assembly of Massachusetts—a rich man, and a very pretty house." At Haverhill he spent Sunday with "some people called Sanders. . . . He made a great fortune by the telephone, and has a beautiful place on a lake out there." And everywhere the essayist admired the dwelling places of the wealthy and the intellectual:

All along the Hudson it is like the rich and finished villas along the Thames by Richmond.

I thought of you at Newport . . . it is the most beautiful sea and sea walk I ever saw in my life; the wooden villas are many of them exquisite too.

[Amherst] is a pretty village near the Connecticut River, with picturesque lines of hill in the landscape. . . . At tea we had exquisite rolls, broiled oysters, and preserved peaches—nothing else—and iced water or tea to wash it down. . . . I had had a great dinner with Phillips Brooks—venison and champagne—the day before.

In the rest of the country, too, culture seemed to be always in possession of the saving remnant, *i.e.,* the richer Anglo-Saxons. For example, a letter and a telegram from General Anderson welcomed him to Richmond, where

. . . we drove to a capital house standing alone, with a large garden behind it; here I found more black servants, and Mrs. Anderson. I was most kindly received. Virginia, of which Richmond is the capital, was colonised not by the Puritans, but by English gentry, and the liking for England and its ways, and for the better sort of English people has never failed. Mrs. Anderson has been an extremely pretty woman; her father was a great planter, who lived in an immense house in the country, with at least a hundred servants, I am told—all blacks. . . . There was a party at dinner, the cloth drawn after dinner in the old English fashion, and excellent Madeira; then we went to the lecture in a tumble-down old hall. . . . My agents were against my coming here, and said I would have no audience, but I had all the "old families," who in general do not go to lectures; one gentleman came in twenty miles on an engine to hear me.

Arnold was asked "to go down and stay at a country house near the sea to shoot duck," and at another "to shoot deer," but his schedule did not permit him to go. Washington, Baltimore, Philadelphia were a glittering galaxy of first families —the Welshes, the MacVeaghs, the Whartons, the Biddles, the Henry Adams', "dear old Bancroft," and "the really best men in Congress," like Senators Bayard, Sherman, and Gibson. At Buffalo there was Mr. Milburn, the leading lawyer, an Englishman: "he is very nice [he was also attorney for the New York Central Railroad] and so is his wife." At Cleveland there was "a charming man to introduce me, Colonel John Hay, who was Lincoln's private secretary." Colonel Hay had just written a violent antilabor novel, *The Breadwinners,* which, in the words of Carl Van Doren, "made a sensation by its defense of property and the old economic order."[13] At Chicago there were the Union Club, General M'Clurg, a literary society, a supper table "splendidly decorated with flowers," and courses from "oysters to ice, with plenty of champagne." In St. Louis, General Sherman, Mr. Hitchcock, "the leading lawyer here," and Mr. Chapman, "a great timber merchant," interested themselves; at Cincinnati "we passed the next day at a beautiful place in the environs, belonging to the daughter of Mr. Longworth, who was long the principal man in Cincinnati"; and, returning through Cleveland, Arnold records that Mrs. John Hay was "an immense heiress."

This kind of hospitality was to be expected, since the British lion could not hide obscurely in hotels. It is perhaps merely unfortunate that in his letters Arnold permits himself a tone of condescension, of uneasy brevity, where other races of men are concerned. He writes, for example, from New York of "the German boys who wait in the hair-cutting room and the clerks at the photographers" who "express their delight at seeing 'a great English poet,' and ask me to write in their autograph books, which they have always ready," but he hurries over this to record at length a compliment from Henry Ward Beecher. In Richmond the great English authority on education refers to schools of colored children as "dem little things," and though he finds the classes "most interesting," he merely remarks in passing that "the Andersons . . . don't yet like their being educated."[14] In St. Louis, where a very small audience comprised "the best of the wealthy and cultivated people," he dismissed the rest of that polyglot metropolis in two sentences: "There is a large population descended from the French of Lou-

<hr />

[13] *The American Novel* (rev. and enl. ed., New York, 1940), p. 197.

[14] As I do not wish to seem to indict Arnold, it is only fair to record that in the same letter (to Mrs. Forster) he says flatly that the Negro children "are neater and better dressed than the Irish scholars in Boston," that the Negro is getting higher wages in the tobacco factories than the poor white, that he could have passed hours in the Negro schools, and that "the dirt, untidiness, and spitting" by whites in the Capitol reminded him "of all that Trollope and Dickens say." *Letters,* II, 287–88.

isiana; their interest is in their priest. There is a large German population; their interest is in their beer-gardens and singing-halls." Indeed, there being a mere three hundred at the lecture, it was painfully obvious that the cultural level of Missouri was low, in sad contrast to that of New England, where "they have been diligent readers of my books for years," where "papa's memory" was "a living power," "the little boys were reading *Tom Brown* with delight," and "all the country places want to hear me on Literature and Science." In New England, more-over, "so many lectures were sold . . . for a fee of 150 dollars before I came . . . that I hardly know what to say."

The general American public were uneasily conscious of a practical discrepancy between the doctrine of disinterested-ness and the appearance of Matthew Arnold for profit under professional lyceum management. It so happened that Lily Langtry arrived in New York a day or two before Arnold for a production of the *School for Scandal.* The New York *World* chronicled this fact without comment on October 15, for news-paper minds understood the necessity a beautiful actress was under to make money. But on the same date the paper quoted an interview in which Matthew Arnold is represented as say-ing: "I am a poor man, and I hope that if I lecture to the Amer-icans they will pay me enough to enable me to retire." Then, after maliciously referring the lecturer to his own words about American vulgarity, the editorial acidly concludes: "it is doubtful if sweetness will melt in his mouth." The Chicago *Tribune* (it is notorious) pictured the lecture tour as an un-worthy search for "filthy lucre." Professor McCallum has dug out of the files of the *Daily Graphic* for November 15 an attack on Arnold by Kate Sanborn for peddling shopworn goods:

Do the American people generally know that Matthew Arnold charges one hundred and fifty dollars[15] per hour for mumbling and stumbling over his printed article on *Literature and Science,* which

[15] It is not clear from Arnold's *Letters* (II, 276) whether $150 was ex-ceptional or standard for his appearance.

appeared in the *Nineteenth Century* of August 1882? We are all willing to pay a dollar to see the man for what he has accomplished and as the son of the noble Rugby master, but isn't it a little cool and cheeky to presume on our ignorance of English magazines?— One of our professors, who spent the whole afternoon before the lecture in carefully reading this article that he might be ready for further information, felt that he had been the victim of a fraud. My "sense of conduct" and my "sense of beauty" were jarred, I confess. As a reader he is a sad failure. He cannot be heard. It must be that he has come to fill his pensioned pockets[16] by showing himself to reverent and admiring crowds. Badly as we need "lucidity," we cannot be helped by his utterances. He does not equal Emerson either in thought or expression.—Are we not entitled to something as yet unpublished when we hear a "lecture"?[17]

At the end of his engagements the New York *Tribune* remarked with heavy irony that Arnold was returning home with "$6000 of the Philistines' money in his pockets." And although the magazines which chiefly circulated among the intellectual classes were not unfriendly, the newspapers—organs of the plain people—pursued the essayist throughout his travels with inimical comment or malicious anecdote.[18]

III

Charges of incompetence and commercialism form a journalistic *argumentum ad hominem* inevitable in the situation but actually irrelevant to the basic problem presented by Arnold's

[16] Just before coming to America Arnold had, after a good deal of hesitation, accepted Gladstone's offer of an annual pension of £250. See Trilling, p. 392.

[17] *New England Quar.*, II, 368.

[18] There is at Yale an unpublished dissertation dealing with American comment on Arnold, which I have not seen. In his *Matthew Arnold's "Sweetness and Light" in America, 1848–1938*, Mr. Seymour Gordden Link says he could find no sectional difference in the newspaper attacks on the author. Even the New England journalists "fairly outdid themselves in poking fun and abuse at the distinguished visitor," and the papers of the Middle West proved the truth of everything Arnold said. (Nashville, George Peabody College for Teachers, 1938. This is an abstract of Mr. Link's thesis.)

ideas. Likewise the easy assertion by editors that American culture was at least no worse than British culture, since Philistinism is a universal trait, was equally facile and equally irrelevant. What the defenders of the democratic culture were really confronting, had they but known it, was a much more fundamental, a much more troublesome, attack, but only Whitman, in his rude colloquial way, phrased the danger precisely. People like Matthew Arnold, he told Traubel in 1888, "make more fuss over foliage than root." "I do not feel myself to be against him in any way," he went on to remark, "but so much is made of the Arnold type of man that we are liable to miss our normal gauge of value." Whitman later expanded this judgment: "The vitiating fact is—the bother of it all is—that men of the Matthew Arnold type dominating contemporary literature judge all men (not literary men alone but all men) by bookish standards." Arnold, he said, "I can never realize . . . we are constitutionally antipathetic: Arnold is porcelain, chinaware, hangings." And with a sardonic richness which only Americans can comprehend Traubel records on a later day concerning Arnold: "It is a great comfort for me to think that the Lord finds a place for them all: and if the Lord can afford to do so, so can we—and not stand off and be critical. We must have the bedbug, the rat, the flea; they all have their places."[19] "I must insist upon the masses, Tom," he told T. B. Harned, "they are our best, they are preservative: I insist upon their integrity as a whole—not, of course, denying or excusing what is bad. Arnold is all wrong on that point: *it is good, not bad, that is common*" (my italics).[20]

---

[19] Horace Traubel, *With Walt Whitman in Camden* (3 vols., New York, 1914–15), I, 95–96, 209; II, 391; III, 121. Even more colloquial is the judgment (III, 400): "my worst criticism would be, that Arnold brings coals to Newcastle—that he brings to the world what the world already has a surfeit of: is rich, hefted, lousy, reeking with delicacy, refinement, elegance, prettiness, propriety, criticism, analysis: *all of them things which threaten to overwhelm us*" (my italics). And, a little later: "Vellum? pshaw! hangings, curtains, finger-bowls, chinaware, Matthew Arnold!" (III, 532)
[20] *Ibid.*, I, 175; *cf.* p. 232. "Arnold always gives you the notion that he

The sensitivity of the poet had discovered what irritated newspapermen had sensed but vaguely; namely, a working interrelation between the Arnoldian doctrine of culture and the Arnoldian belief in racial snobbery and anti-democratic political action.[21] He had said, to be sure, that England needed more quality rather than less; that culture is the study of perfection; and that culture "seeks to do away with classes; to make the best that has been thought and known in the world current," but the doing away with classes proves not to mean what it seems to mean. Though he had written that "France has organised democracy with a certain indisputable grandeur and success," that was in the sixties; in the eighties he published a succession of pessimistic estimates of democratic government.[22] After denying again in 1880, as he had formerly denied, the doctrine of natural rights,[23] he pictured a possible "last scene in the wonderful career of Lord Beaconsfield," in which that

hates to touch the dirt—the dirt is so dirty! But everything comes out of the dirt—everything: everything comes out of the people, the everyday people, the people as you find them and leave them: not university people, not F. F. V. people: people, people, just people!"

[21] The tendency to see Arnold as all of a piece, arising from the failure to differentiate his social theory before the Second Reform Bill from the reactionary views he expressed in the eighties, vitiates most of the interpretative studies. Students of Arnold have also in the main failed to study the changes of text between the first appearance of an essay or lecture in the magazines and its later appearance in volume form, and they have signally failed to study the uncollected essays. In his *Victorian Critics of Democracy* (Minneapolis, 1938) Mr. Benjamin Evans Lippincott gives a full analytical view of an orthodox sort (pp. 93–133) but fails to realize how deeply the Hyde Park "riots" and the Franco-Prussian War affected Arnold. The only genetic study of Arnold's political development that has weight seems to be that of Otto Elias, *Matthew Arnolds politische Grundanschauungen* (Palaestra, No. 175); (Leipzig, 1931).

[22] "The Future of Liberalism," *Nineteenth Century*, VIII (July 1880), 1–18, collected in *Irish Essays;* "Numbers" (already discussed); "The Nadir of Liberalism," *Nineteenth Century*, XIX (May 1886), 645–63; "The Zenith of Conservatism," *ibid.*, XXI (Jan. 1887), 148–64; "Up to Easter," *ibid.*, XXI (May 1887), 629–43; "From Easter to August," *ibid.*, XXII (Sept. 1887), 310–24.

[23] "Not that there is . . . any natural right in every man to the possession of a vote, or any gift of wisdom and virtue conferred by such possession." "The Future of Liberalism," *Works*, 15 vols. (London, 1903–4), XI, 140.

118

octogenarian, in a field-marshal's uniform, enters the House of Commons and commands the speaker to "take away that bauble," the mace. In 1886 he wrote that there was little hope in the "Parliamentary mind," that Gladstone was a "mere parliamentarian," and that "the danger of our situation is so grave that it can hardly be exaggerated." In 1887 he said that "parliaments, parties, and politicians, are more or less discredited," that "plain, reasonable people throughout the country" look upon the House of Commons "with ever deepening disgust and shame," and that "it is a relief to them when Parliament is not sitting; they are uneasy and apprehensive as soon as it meets again, for they know that the time for humiliation has returned." In his penultimate article he wrote that "long ago the country had made up its mind that to pretend 'discussion' to be the object of such debates as those which have gone on in the House of Commons during the last few years was an absurdity," expressed pleasure in the adoption of a stringent cloture rule, and argued that "dangerous expressions" ought to be suppressed by force. In his last article he pictured democracy as "feather-brained" because it thinks "restraint a curse, and doing as one likes the height of felicity" ("The Americans in general think so too"); prophesied inevitable riots, "roughs, drink, fires, and bloodshed" in England unless there was radical political change; called Gladstone a "stump orator" whose "powers of self-deception are so inexhaustible that he is never insincere," and charged him with stirring up class hatreds. The fact that Arnold had the Fenian movement under his eyes does not alter the destructive character of comments like these.[24] In

[24] "We had the obstructed and paralysed House of Commons. Then, finally came the news one morning of the London street-mobs and street-riots, heightening yet further the impression of our impotence and disarray. The recent trial and acquittal of the mob-orators will probably complete it." "I agree, too, that the House of Commons is a scandal, and Ireland a crying danger. I agree that monster processions and monster meetings in the public streets and parks are the letting out of anarchy, and that our weak dealing with them is deplorable." "The Nadir of Liberalism," *Nineteenth Century,* XIX, 646, 647.

contrast to either Gladstone or Disraeli he set up Bismarck as his model statesman because "those legitimate needs and that security of Germany, which thirty years ago seemed unattainable for her, he has attained. Germany, which thirty years ago was hampered, weak, and in low esteem, is now esteemed, strong, and with her powers all at command. It was a great object and the great *Reichskanzler* has attained it."[25]

The smooth surface of the doctrine of "culture" has drawn attention away from the deep distrust of the people upon which it rests. Neither the aristocracy, the middle class, nor the proletariat is fit to govern England, three categories which practically exhaust the population of Great Britain, except for a saving remnant; yet by the eighties this remnant has mysteriously grown into a body of "plain, reasonable people" who, standing outside of political action, are somehow to prevent the state from becoming a "feather-brained democracy!" Like Lindbergh, Arnold in his later years pretended to be outside politics, said that he disliked political subjects, and hinted mysteriously that he was speaking, he hoped (or feared), for the last time.[26] His equalitarianism is purely theoretic. The

---

[25] *Ibid.,* XIX, 649. In 1865 he had been torn between his disgust with the lack of aristocratic refinement in Germany, where the "whole middle class hates refinement and disbelieves in it," and his admiration for "Bismarck's audacity, resolution, and success," in contrast to Palmerston. Most of the English, he then thought, were about on Palmerston's level. *Letters,* I, 354, 356. Arnold early expressed an enthusiastic admiration for the "clearness and width of view," the "energy and precision of Napoleon III." *Ibid.,* I, 11–12.

[26] The openings of the late uncollected essays are all in this tone; *e.g.,* in "Up to Easter" he says it is only his desire to be useful that brings him into politics, that he knows "the impatience and irritation which my intervention in these matters causes to many people. Nothing I should like better than to feel assured that I should never have occasion to write a line on politics again." Politics are "a mass of insincerity, of phrase, fiction, and claptrap, which can impose, one would think, on no plain reasonable man outside of politics," and thousands of plain, reasonable people "want nothing for themselves in politics" and "only demand that the politician shall not bring the country into danger and disaster." *Nineteenth Century,* XXI, 629–30. The identification of all political action with chicanery and the creation of a bloc theoretically "non-political," of which Arnold is the

magazine version of *Culture and Anarchy* was, except for the first part (an Oxford Lecture), originally entitled *Anarchy and Authority,* Arnold being heavily enlisted on the side of authority, as a passage omitted from all but the first versions of the work amply testifies:

With me, indeed, this rule of conduct is hereditary. I remember my father, in one of his unpublished letters, written more than forty years ago, when the political and social state of the country was gloomy and troubled and there were riots in many places, goes on, after strongly insisting on the badness and foolishness of the government, and on the harm and dangerousness of our feudal and aristocratical constitution of society, and ends thus: "As for rioting, the old Roman way of dealing with that is always the right one; flog the rank and file, and fling the ringleaders from the Tarpeian Rock!" And this opinion we can never forsake.[27]

The occasion of the famous essay was the mild rioting in Hyde Park, consequent upon the first defeat of the Second Reform Bill; Arnold then, as always, inferred the direst consequences from mob actions.[28] In 1859 he had joined the Queen's Westminster Rifles because he thought the nation was in need of control by force;[29] he thought "the great States of the Continent have two great elements of cohesion" lacking in England, "their administrative system and . . . their army";[30] while lamenting the breakdown of parliamentary government in the eighties, he dwelt also upon the dangers of "Jacobinism": "It is small, but it is active and visible. It is a sinister apparition. We know

---

spokesman, is a familiar device in propaganda directed against democratic processes.

[27] *Cornhill Magazine,* XVIII (Aug. 1868), 250. In *Culture and Anarchy* this is omitted, and one reads: "without order there can be no society, and without society there can be no human perfection. And this opinion we can never forsake, etc."

[28] The *Letters* are illuminating. See the accounts in I, 389–90, 438.

[29] ". . . it seems to me that the establishment of these Rifle Corps will more than ever throw the power into the hands of the upper and middle classes, and these classes will thus have over the lower classes the superiority, not only of wealth and intelligence, which they have now, but of physical force." *Letters,* I, 126.

[30] *Ibid.,* I, 440.

its works from having seen them so abundantly in France; it has the temper of hatred and the aim of destruction. There are two varieties of Jacobin, the hysterical Jacobin, and the pedantic Jacobin; we possess both, and both are dangerous."[31] And he alternated between denouncing the brutality and violence of labor and flattering the English peasantry as being more "patient, faithful, respectful, kindly" than any other peasantry whatsoever.[32] The Irish peasantry, however, not being respectful or kindly, were to be controlled by force,[33] and the Conservative government was encouraged to suppress freedom of assembly, freedom of speech, and freedom of the press in Ireland.[34]

I V

There was, to be sure, a kindly and likable side to Arnold, whose views of education were extraordinarily philosophic, who set his face against the laissez-faire economic philosophy of the middle class, who saw the absurdity and narrowness of many Protestant sects, and whose theory of culture, in its broader aspects, is both useful and comprehensive. But a man to whom utterances like the foregoing easily came was essentially a Hamiltonian, whose character, perceptions, and sympathies fitted in easily with that of the dominant groups

[31] *Nineteenth Century,* XIX, 654.

[32] On the frequency with which Arnold identifies the working class with brutality and violence see Lippincott, *op. cit.* The passage on the English peasantry is in the *Nineteenth Century,* XIX, 653.

[33] Arnold perpetually insists on one law for both England and Ireland and on the enforcement of this law by administrative action. Force bills directed against Ireland had his entire support; and he wrote explicitly: "In general, administrative action is what is now required against anarchy in Ireland, *not recourse to proceedings at law"* (my italics). *Ibid.,* XXI, 159. And though he said it was the duty of government to cure injustice, let us never "approve of its leaving the other part of its duty, the quelling of anarchy, undone" (p. 160).

[34] "There are surely some kinds of speeches, some kinds of meetings, some kinds of newspaper-writing, which in the present circumstances of Ireland should not be permitted there and should be stopped." *Ibid.,* XXI, 159.

in the United States. He was never tired of quoting Charles Sumner's statement that what had particularly struck him in England was the large class of gentlemen as distinct from the nobility, gentlemen of "serious knowledge, high accomplishment, and refined taste." With these gentlemen England abounded; and in view of Arnold's assertions that the English nobility was politically bankrupt, that an aristocratic society in the broadest sense is the most desirable society, and that a "high standard of civilisation" can therefore be maintained only by the gentlemen class, the implication was irresistible: standards of civilization in the United States could be maintained only by gentlemen. Whoever the American gentleman might be, it was clear who he was not—he was not a member of the great, dreary middle class but a spirit sufficiently delicate and rare to appreciate Arnold's statement: "in America, perhaps, we see the disadvantage of having a social equality before there has been any such high standard of social life and manners formed."[35] And that the gentleman must perforce spring from Anglo-Saxon stock was an inference to be drawn from the unfortunate spread of a moral equalitarianism in France:

The sense in France for the power of conduct has not greatly deepened. . . . The sense for the power of intellect and knowledge has not been adequate either. The sense for beauty has not been adequate. Intelligence and beauty have been, in general, but so far reached, as they can be and are reached by men, who of the elements of perfect humanisation, lay thorough hold upon one only,— the power of social intercourse and manners. . . . Well then, if a nation laying no sufficient hold upon the powers of beauty and knowledge, and a most failing and feeble hold upon the power of conduct, comes to demoralisation and intellectual stoppage and fearful troubles, we need not be inordinately surprised.[36]

The inference was driven home by a significant paragraph in the essay on "Democracy," which was originally the preface to Arnold's report on French schools:

[35] "Equality," *Works*, X, 65.
[36] *Ibid.*, X, 72.

The greatest men of America, her Washingtons, Hamiltons, Madisons, well understanding that aristocratical institutions are not in all times and places possible; well perceiving that in their Republic there was no place for these; comprehending, therefore, that from these that security for national dignity and greatness, an ideal commanding popular reverence, was not to be obtained, but knowing that this ideal was indispensable, would have been rejoiced to found a substitute for it in the dignity and authority of the State. They deplored the weakness and insignificance of the executive power as a calamity. When the inevitable course of events has made our self-government something really like that of America, when it has removed or weakened that security for national dignity, which we possessed in *aristocracy,* will the substitute of the *State* be equally wanting to us? If it is, then the dangers of America will really be ours; the dangers which come from the multitude being in power, with no adequate ideal to elevate or guide the multitude.[37]

Franklin and Jefferson are absent from this list; and it is significant that in a sentence later added to the essay, Arnold uses the word "Americanise" in a pejorative sense:

On what action may we rely to replace, for some time at any rate, that action of the aristocracy upon the people of this country, which we have seen exercise an influence in many respects elevating and beneficial, but which is rapidly, and from inevitable causes, ceasing? In other words, and to use a short and significant modern expression which everyone understands, what influence may help us to prevent the English people from becoming, with the growth of democracy, *Americanised?* On the action of the State.[38]

"Americanisation" was something opposed to culture, but the American gentleman could neatly sidestep the implicit dilemma by adopting, upon Arnold's recommendation, two con-

---

[37] *Ibid.,* X, 25–26.
[38] *Ibid.,* X, 22–23. Dr. Elias notes that the passage first appeared in 1861 in the introduction to "Popular Education of France," but fails to notice the illuminating fact that the sentence about being "Americanised" was added some twenty years later. *Cf.* also p. 38, where one reads that if the middle class do not adopt state education, they will "Americanise" England; *i.e.,* "rule it by their energy, but . . . deteriorate it by their low ideals and want of culture."

tradictory theories: he was to avoid the contamination of "democratic" action, especially political action, if he possibly could; and yet he was to put his faith in a mysteriously perfected "state" action—presumably action by gentlemen for gentlemen without reference to "the growth of democracy." It is not without meaning that Arnold described the old, unreformed American Senate as "perhaps, of all the institutions of that country, the most happily devised, the most successful in its working."[39] The Senate which thus aroused Arnold's enthusiasm has been less enthusiastically called the most exclusive rich men's club in the world.

Waited upon by lesser races,[40] secure in the faith that wealth "is conceived as a thing which almost any American may attain, and which almost every American will use respectably," the American gentleman might also take pride in the fact that in one respect he was ahead of his English brethren. He did not live in a country where it was necessary to introduce a bill "to prevent the land of a man who dies intestate from going, as it goes now, to his eldest son," a custom giving the "almost exclusive possession of the land of this country" to the Barbarians.[41] Secure therefore in his easy economic righteousness, he could refrain from meddling with "machinery," serenely trusting a "best self" which would mysteriously unite him with other gentlemen, reading in Arnold that "We are in no peril from giving authority to this, because it is the truest friend we all of us can have; and when anarchy is a danger to us, to this authority we may turn with sure trust."

For this "best self," it seems, "inspires faith, and is capable of affording a serious principle of authority," as the Duke of Wellington prophetically saw. Remote from the meaninglessness of political life, the American gentleman could discover in this undefined "best self" a union with other Hamiltonians:

[39] *Civilization in the United States,* p. 143.
[40] "Their domestic service is done for them by Irish, Germans, Swedes, negroes." *Ibid.,* p. 120.
[41] See the section on "Our Liberal Practitioners" in *Culture and Anarchy.*

So whatever brings risk of tumult and disorder, multitudinous processions in the streets of our crowded towns, multitudinous meetings in their public places and parks,—demonstrations perfectly unnecessary in the present course of affairs,—our best self, or right reason, plainly enjoins us to set our faces against. It enjoins us to encourage and uphold the occupants of the executive power, whoever they may be, in firmly prohibiting them. But it does this clearly and resolutely, and is thus a real principle of authority, because it does it with a free conscience; because in thus provisionally, strengthening the executive power, it knows that it . . . is establishing *the State,* or organ of our collective best self, of our national right reasons.[42]

And in the Newport villas and the clubs gentlemen could congratulate themselves on having an authoritative word in their favor: "Certainly equality will never of itself alone give us a perfect civilisation."[43] Did they perhaps also agree that Grant "had governing instincts"?[44]

[42] The reader is entreated to consider the whole argument of "Doing as One Likes" in *ibid.*

[43] *Works,* X, 91. The fact that the next sentence says that British inequality will not produce a perfect civilization simply flatters American vanity.

[44] *Civilization in the United States,* p. 43. Arnold says that Grant admired the South "for the boldness with which they silenced all opposition and all croaking by press or by individuals within their control."

Thoreau as Moralist

Prepared for the centennial of Thoreau's death and published under the title "Thoreau and Human Nature" in *The Atlantic Monthly*, Vol. CCX (September 1962), 56–61.

ON Sunday, May 5, 1962, with appropriate ceremony Henry David Thoreau was, on the centenary of his death, formally admitted to the Hall of Fame in New York City. To his admirers over the world this seemed not only an appropriate action, but an action too long delayed. If Thoreau has not exerted an influence quite comparable to that of James Fenimore Cooper or Edgar Allan Poe, he has exerted an international influence that has increased in the twentieth century; and this influence, moreover, has been an influence of action, as in India or among our own Freedom Riders, and not an influence solely of literature and thought. It will in no way reflect upon the justice of his admission or upon the good sense of the jury that selected Thoreau to speculate on what he might have said, were he alive today and aware of the honor.

He hated cities, he hated museums, and he hated statuary. In September, 1843, he wrote in his journal: "I walked through New York yesterday—and met no real or living person." In another, undated entry in a notebook he said: "I hate museums; there is nothing so weighs upon my spirits. They are the catacombs of nature." And in 1859 when somebody asked him to subscribe for a statue to Horace Mann, he declined, thinking that a man "ought not any more to take up room in the world after he was dead. . . . It is very offensive to my

127

imagination to see the dying stiffen into statues at this rate."
Eulogies and statuary are perhaps necessary, however, and one
may hope they are the outward and visible sign of an inward
and spiritual grace.

I am not a Thoreau specialist. I am not expert in Thoreau's
reading, which was immense, nor in his economic views, if he
had any, nor in his love life, which seems to have been meager
and problematical, nor have I participated in the battle—dare
one say, of the ants?—that has raged over the exact location
of the famous hut on Walden Pond. But what does one find
on re-reading Thoreau?

One general image it is difficult to confirm. I can best express
this image by citing two sentences with which Leo Stoller
begins his study of Thoreau's economic views. He writes:
"Henry Thoreau is the man who lived alone in a hut by Walden Pond and went to jail rather than pay taxes. Such, at any
rate, is the thumbnail sketch of him by an America eager to tol-
erate what it considers primitivism and oddity." Mr. Stoller
does not say this image is correct; he merely gives it as a sketch
of popular belief. Neither branch of the legend seems to be
quite true. Thoreau went to jail only once for failing to pay his
taxes; he did not protest when they were paid for him; and Sam
Staples, the town jailer, said he was mad as the devil for being
locked up.

As for living an eremite's life in a sort of primitive wilderness by Walden, this, too, will not quite do. Thoreau went
there July 4, 1845, and it was theoretically his home for two
years and three months. But he had to abandon it from
Wednesday, November 12, to Saturday, December 6, because,
not having plastered the hut in warm weather, he had to
go home until the plaster had slowly dried. During the second
summer he took a by no means solitary trip to the Maine
woods. In good weather he went to Concord almost daily, sometimes lingering there into the night, going either to look after

his family and see his friends or to do odd jobs for pay. In good weather, likewise, he was frequently visited by friends, neighbors, transcendentalists, curiosity seekers, and even young ladies. In the winter he had the companionship of the ice-cutters and occasionally of ice fishermen, which he seems to have enjoyed, and in the fall, particularly, of hunters, one group of whom he characterizes as a "numerous and merry crew."

Of the eighteen chapters into which *Walden* is divided, the first and longest, entitled "Economy" (in the Greek sense) is as much social commentary as it is directions how to build a cabin and plant beans. Another (VI) is entitled "Visitors." Another (X) describes a visit to the Baker farm and chronicles a chat with its inhabitants. A third (VIII) is called "The Village," "that desperate, odd-fellow society," he calls it. Chapter XIV is a kind of Robert Frost commentary upon present and former residents and frequenters of the area. One scholarly editor of *Walden* insists that Chapter IV, on "Sounds," may be a lesson in how to read the universal, living language of Nature. I am not disposed to dispute this philosophical assertion or to pretend to be deaf to the native woodnotes wild held suspended in its exquisitely modulated prose.

But of the twenty-two paragraphs that make up the chapter, nine are devoted to or occasioned by the noises made by the railroad trains, one has to do with the "faint rattle of a carriage or team along the distant highway," one is occasioned by hearing the church bells of Lincoln, Acton, Bedford and Concord, one combines the distant lowing of a cow with a satirical passage on some village lads singing, the penultimate paragraph begins with another distant rumbling of wagons over bridges, the baying of farm dogs, and the lowing of another (?) cow, and the final one opens with a meditation on crowing roosters, a sound, says Thoreau, heard round the world, even on sailing ships. Sounds are sounds, and aural acuity —Thoreau had sensitive ears—can be as well displayed by recording the rumble of a team over a bridge as by recording the language of an aldermanic frog as tr-r-r-oonk, tr-r-r-oonk, tr-r-r-oonk, but the ordinary reader may be forgiven if he is baffled when told that this not very original onomatopoeia is a new lesson in the universal, living language of Nature.

I note also with mild amusement that Chapter V, entitled "Solitude," contains phrases like these: "I find that visitors have been there," "I was frequently notified of the passage of a traveller along the highway sixty rods off by the scent of his pipe," "some came from the village to fish for pouts," "men frequently say to me," "I one evening overtook one of my townsmen." Wiser than specialists, Thoreau says flatly in *Walden* that we belong to the community. I think he went to Walden Pond in part to get away from his garrulous mother, and to meditate and write; but he was no solitary Alexander Selkirk, no monarch of all he surveyed, no Robinson Crusoe discovering with astonishment on the sand a print of a human foot, no Trappist monk dedicated to silence, no St. Anthony trying to be holy in the desert. He made his hut and he lived in it because it was fun to do so. I have known Vermonters who lived far more solitary lives in far more lonely dwellings.

A man maun gang his ain gait, as the Scotch say, without being a solitary in either the romantic or the religious sense. On re-reading other books by Thoreau, I am astonished to see how large a fraction of their bulk is devoted to commentary on humanity. *A Week on the Concord and Merrimack Rivers* runs to 518 pages, of which about 200 have to do directly with the journeying. Both streams run—and ran—through territory long since subdued to human needs, and the pages deal with farm and church, canal and bridge, lock and village, factory and stage-coach, river commerce and social history. He or his brother ever and again hails canalboat men or farmers or small boys or lock-keepers or hospitable farmwives. Their little trip, in itself charming, was quite without wildness, and could be described in good set Victorian terms as the lazy tour of two idle apprentices. For wildness, one has to turn to Kinglake's *Eothen,* or Frémont's *Report of the Exploring Expedition to the Rocky Mountains,* or Parkman's *The Oregon Trail,* or Melville's *Typee,* all more or less contemporary with the *Week.* Thoreau's harmless camp-outs contrast sharply with Bartram's desperate struggle to preserve his boat and his gear from alligators in Florida. The *Week* is no worse for not recording dangers of scalping by Indians or being imprisoned by fanatical Bedouins or being eaten by cannibals, but it is as it is, a volume diversified with essays on Chaucer, local history, the nature and function of poetry, the working of friendship, the nature of time, the truth of Neo-Platonism, a whimsical theory of deserts, the effects of music upon the soul, Huguenots on Staten Island, Pythagoreanism, and the literary style of Sir Walter Raleigh. I am not trying to find fault with the *Week;* I am merely trying to define its warm humanity, which has only a secondary relation to natural philosophy, as one will realize if he compares it to Muir's *The Mountains of California,* or Clarence King's *Mountaineering in the Sierras,* or even the far more domesticated *King Solomon's Ring* of Konrad Lorenz, in all of which scientific considerations are vertebrate and central to the prose.

It has been remarked that Wordsworth does not read very convincingly in the tropics; and when Henry Thoreau had really to confront the savagery of nature, even in a relatively limited degree, he found that the warm humanism he could impute to natural sights and sounds in eastern Massachusetts was not universal or relevant. Nothing is more illuminating than the mood of cosmic bewilderment that overcame him after his ascent of Mount Katahdin, as recorded in *The Maine Woods:*

Some part of the beholder, even some vital part, seems to escape through the loose grating of his ribs as he ascends. He is more lone than you can imagine. There is less of substantial thought and fair understanding in him than in the plains where men inhabit. His reason is dispersed and shadowy, more thin and subtle, like the air.

Vast, Titanic, inhuman Nature has got him at disadvantage, caught him alone, and pilfers him of some of his divine faculty. She does not smile on him as in the plains. She seems to say sternly, Why came ye here before your time. This ground is not prepared for you. . . . The tops of the mountains are among the unfinished parts of the globe, whither it is a slight insult to the gods to climb and pry into their secrets, and try their effect on our humanity. Only daring and insolent men, perchance, go there. Simple races, as savages, do not climb mountains—their tops are sacred and mysterious tracts never visited by them.

And, some six pages later:

This was that Earth of which we have heard, made out of Chaos and Old Night. Here was no man's garden, but the unhandseled globe. It was no lawn, nor pasture, nor mead, nor woodland, nor lea, nor arable, nor waste land. It was the fresh and natural surface of the planet Earth, as it was made forever and ever. . . . Man was not to be associated with it. It was Matter, vast, terrific—not his Mother Earth that we have heard of, nor for him to tread on, or to be buried in,—no, it were being too familiar even to let his bones lie there,—the home, this, of Necessity and Fate.

There is more to the passage, all in the same tone. This, clearly, is not cosmic comfort but cosmic scare. It suggests that for Thoreau, as for Wordsworth, Nature is in the temperate zone, always not far from the clearing, and has its meaning principally in terms of man.

Man is rather more central to Thoreau's interest, despite the endless pages of natural lore in the *Journals,* than some schools of interpretation are prepared to admit. This truth is the more strongly suggested when we contrast some of the books brought out within three or four years of his death, with the four volumes of extracts on nature from the *Journals,* published by H. G. O. Blake about a quarter of a century afterward. Thus *A Yankee in Canada* is virtually a sociological report on French-Canadian life; and not even Thoreau's curiosity about the falls in the rivers of Canada dislocates the centrality of the theme of Canadian culture. *The Maine Woods* has, I think, two major interests, one of which is the actual life of white man and red man in the woods or in the clearings, and the processes of their existence; and the other is Indian psychology, especially the psychology of Joseph Polis, of which the "Allegash and East Branch" section of the book is a lengthy exposition in biographical form.

Thoreau's interest in processes is an important element in the volume. A long passage on the New England Friction Match Company, a description of the McCauslin clearing, the way Joe Polis killed, skinned, and cut up a moose, the account of the Ansel Smith place (as circumstantial as a Sears Roebuck catalogue), the way the guide set up camp, the way Joe Polis carried a canoe, the way Henry Thoreau located his lost companion—these passages of circumstantial observation of human behavior make us understand why, two-thirds of the way through the book, Thoreau writes:

Wild as it was, it was hard for me to get rid of the association of the settlements. Any deadly and monotonous sound, to which I did not distinctly attend, passed for a sound of human industry. The waterfalls which I heard were not without their dams and mills to my imagination,—and several times I found that I had been regarding the steady rushing sound of the wind from over the woods beyond the rivers as that of a train of cars,—the cars of Quebec.

Even his magnificent description of the desolation wrought by flooding a lake draws from him a civic comparison to the "wharves of the largest city in the world, decayed, and the earth and planking washed away," just before they reach the safe haven of the Chamberlain farm.

As for that remarkable book, *Cape Cod,* who can forget the human drama of the shipwreck at Cohasset, the vivid account of the Wellfleet oysterman and his family, the memorable descriptions of Provincetown, or the shrewd remark that the Pilgrims possessed few of the qualities of the pioneer: "They did not go at once into the woods with their axes. They were a family and a church, and were more anxious to keep together, though it were on the sand, than to explore and colonize a

New World." Thoreau's book is a close examination of how it is possible to live in an area so barren that the author several times "refrained from asking the inhabitants for a string or a piece of wrapping-paper, for fear I should rob them." The landscape, or rather the seascape, is wonderfully described, but the problem is the environment as a setting for human existence, not, as on the top of Mount Katahdin, the landscape as a denial of human validity.

One is grateful for serious studies of Thoreau and transcendentalism, Thoreau and Oriental thought, Thoreau and the classics, Thoreau and the Harvard library, Thoreau and politics, and much else of this kind. I venture to suggest, however, that the topic of Thoreau and human nature is still a central theme. There is a wonderful episode in Volume V of the *Journals* (the entry is dated May 31, 1853) in which Thoreau tries to get George Melvin to tell him where he found the *Azalea nudiflora,* which reads as if it were written in prose by Robert Frost. George Melvin was not going to give in easily; whereupon Thoreau says, "Well, I told him he had better tell me where it was; I was a botanist and ought to know." Channing had almost stumbled upon the secret place but hadn't found it, and the entry runs: " 'Channing,' he said, 'came close by it once, when it was in flower. He thought he'd surely find it then; but he didn't, and he said nothing to him.' " Melvin, Thoreau and the dog finally go to the spot. We have this characteristic bit of Yankee psychology: "[Melvin] showed me how near Channing came. ('You won't tell him what I said; will you?' said he.) I offered to pay him for his trouble, but he wouldn't take anything. He had just as lief I'd know as not. He thought it first came out last Wednesday, on the 25th."

Or take this wonderful description of the drunken Dutchman in the *Journals* for 1850 (II:49–51), which I condense:

Getting into Patchogue late one night in an oyster-boat, there was a drunken Dutchman aboard whose wit reminded me of Shakespeare. When we came to leave the beach, our boat was aground, and we

134

were detained three hours waiting for the tide. In the meanwhile two of the fishermen took an extra dram at the beach house. Then they stretched themselves on the seaweed by the shore in the sun to sleep off the effects of their debauch. One was an inconceivably broad-faced young Dutchman,—but oh! of such a peculiar breadth and heavy look. I should not know whether to call it more ridiculous or sublime. . . . For the whole voyage they lay flat on their backs on the bottom of the boat, in the bilge-water and wet with each bailing, half insensible and wallowing in their vomit. But ever and anon, when aroused by the rude kicks or curses of the skipper, the Dutchman, who never lost his wit nor equanimity, though snoring and rolling in the vomit produced by his debauch, blurted forth some happy repartee like an illuminated swine. It was the earthiest, slimiest wit I ever heard. The countenance was one of a million. . . . When we were groping up the narrow creek of Patchogue at ten o'clock at night, keeping our boat off, now from this bank, now from that . . . the two inebriates roused themselves betimes. . . . The Dutchman gave wise directions to the steerer. . . . Suddenly rousing himself up where the sharpest-eyed might be bewildered in the darkness, he leaned over the side of the boat and pointed straight down into the creek, averring that that identical hole was a first-rate place for eels. And again he roused himself at the right time and declared what luck he had once had with his pots . . . in another place, which we were floating over in the dark. At last he suddenly stepped on to another boat which was moored to the shore, with a divine ease and sureness, saying, "Well, good-night, take care of yourselves, I can't be with you any longer." He was one of the few remarkable men whom I have met. . . . When I said, "You have had a hard time of it to-day," he answered with indescribable good humor out of the midst of his debauch, with watery eyes, "Well, it doesn't happen every day."

We rub our eyes. Is this the Henry Thoreau who sought in vain for a hound, a bayhorse, and a turtledove, or is it a picture by Hogarth or Teniers sympathetically translated out of pigment into prose?

Our histories of American literature are deficient in a number of categories. They seldom or never, for example, recognize the greatness of American biographical writing, which, beginning before Cotton Mather and extending to our own

135

time, has given us masterpieces by Parton, Gamaliel Bradford, Douglas Southall Freeman, and others. They scarcely know what to do with most non-fictional prose, whether of the informal essay type, of political theory, or of science; and to read in them one would, in many cases, never learn that writers like Samuel Leonard, Daniel Dulany, John C. Calhoun, or Herbert Croly in one category, or James Wilson, Matthew Fountain Maury, Isaac Ray, or Louis Agassiz in the other, ever lived in the United States. They do not know what to do with the powerful library of travel literature written by Americans like John C. Frémont, John Wesley Powell, Isaac L. Stevens, Frederick Law Olmstead, or George B. Catlin—books that are catalogued in these histories but never analyzed as works of literary art. But I think the greatest deficiency in these manuals is their failure to recognize the existence of that type of writer the French call the moralist. For him American literary criticism has small space.

With us the moral is always equated with the didactic; and, properly, we flee from writing that has too palpable a design upon us. But the great moralists of the ancient world like Cato, Theophrastus and Plutarch, the great moralists of Europe —Machiavelli, Montaigne, La Rochefoucauld, Pascal, Lichtenberg, Voltaire, Vauvenargues—and our own Franklin and Emerson are not thus childishly to be dismissed.

When Lichtenberg writes:

First there is a time when we believe everything without reasons. Then, for a short time, we believe discriminatingly. Then we believe nothing at all. And then we believe everything again and, indeed, cite reasons why we believe everything;

when La Rochefoucauld writes:

There is often more pride than kindness in our pitying the misfortunes of our enemies; we give them proofs of our compassionateness to bring home to them our superiority;

when Pascal writes:

Men never do evil so completely and cheerfully as when they do it from religious conviction;

136

when Voltaire writes:

I have never made but one prayer to God, a very short one: "O Lord, make my enemies ridiculous." And God granted it;

when Emerson writes:

I have heard with admiring submission the experience of the lady who declared that the sense of being perfectly well-dressed gives a feeling of inward tranquillity which religion is powerless to bestow,

we know in each case that we are in the hands of some one who has profound observations to make about human nature. Such *sententiae* are not epigrams in the modern sense, though they may be in the Greek meaning of the term, and they rise above mere brilliance in proportion as they make us feel their authors are men of sagacity, writers who have seen ". . . cities of men / And manners, climates, councils, governments," themselves not least, but honored of them all. They have probed motives, analyzed actions, distinguished between the specious and the real; and they have been led to their generalizations partly by the love of an art that prefers condensation to expansiveness, and partly by a passionate interest in human character.

In an admirable little essay, Louis Kronenberger (who, to be sure, tends to the view that the great moralists of the past are mostly persons of birth, blood, and breeding) has defined the work of the moralist. He writes:

What they did, systematically and untiringly, is gaze back and forth from their fellow-beings to themselves. From what they themselves are thinking, they postulate their neighbors' thoughts; from what they crave, they deduce their neighbors' desires; from what they themselves would conceal, they infer their neighbors' dissemblings. The province of this great line of aphorists is worldly existence; men and women; real-life masks and mummers; a way of life, moreover, that involves and that instructs the self. . . . Accordingly, as they studied the human countenance, they would note something masklike or unduly bland about it, or too set about its smile; or, having the good luck to steal up on it unawares, they noted a look of hate or envy in the eyes, or of something bitter about the mouth. And as they peered into the human heart—not least their own—they

137

would spy out much they had for a long time shunned, much else they have never suspected.

Hence, he argues, their frequent skepticism, even the cynicism of their thought. I think the great moralists have frequently been persons of established social positions, but they are not all necessarily so. I suggest that the most illuminating sentence in Mr. Kronenberger's paragraph is the first one: "What they did, systematically and untiringly, is gaze back and forth from their fellow-beings to themselves." And this is a definition of Henry Thoreau when he considers mankind.

Thoreau is one of the great moralists in the French sense. In his apothegms, his pithy paragraphs on human behavior, we more frequently find that quality Lowell praised in Thoreau's writing: "The style is compact and the language has an antique purity like wine grown colorless with age." He labored to perfect a lapidary effect. In 1851 the *Journals* contain this passage, striking and profound: "It is the fault of some excellent writers—De Quincey's first impressions on seeing London suggest it to me—that they express themselves with too great fullness and detail. They give the most faithful, natural and life-like account of their sensations, mental and physical, but they lack moderation and sententiousness." Later that same year he spoke of "sentences uttered with your back to the wall," and the next year he said: "The peculiarity of a work of genius is the absence of the speaker from his speech." A little before he quit his journal he wrote: "The fruit a thinker bears is *sentences,*—statements or opinions." Sententiousness—the creating of the rhetorical form known as the *sententia*—is, I think, one of the unique achievements in Thoreau. Whereas his pages on nature tend to be loose and repetitive, his writing about man is commonly tight and condensed. We have had a small library of books on nature out of Thoreau; we lack a good book on human nature in Thoreau.

I find the key of this writing in an entry for June 15, 1840, in the *Journals:* "Why always insist that men incline to the moral side of their being? Our life is not all moral. Surely, its actual phenomena deserve to be studied impartially. The science of Human Nature has never been attempted, as the science of Nature has. The dry light has ever shone on it. Neither physics nor metaphysics have touched it." It is not necessary to determine whether this is a transcendental remark in order to comprehend the special quality of Thoreau as an observer of humanity.

The subject is difficult for the critic to handle because all our attempts to force Thoreau into a system are as futile as the same attempt is with respect to Montaigne or La Rochefoucauld. Consider, however, these striking *sententiae* culled from the pages of Thoreau's *Journals:*

Man is the artificer of his own happiness.

The words of some men are thrown forcibly against you and adhere like burrs.

We may well neglect many things, provided we overlook them.

Nothing was ever so unfamiliar and startling to me as my own thoughts.

The man of principle never gets a holiday.

There must be some narrowness in the soul that compels one to have secrets.

Any reverence, even for a material thing, proceeds from an elevation of character.

The imagination never forgives an insult.

Each of these compels one to think. But to what system of thought shall they be referred?

Sometimes Thoreau's *sententiae* have a Voltairean tone, as in the following:

Read the Englishman's history of the French and Indian wars, and then read the Frenchman's, and see how each awards the meed of glory to the other's monsters of cruelty or perfidy.

One man lies in his words, and gets a bad reputation; another in his manners, and enjoys a good one.

Beauty and true wealth are always thus cheap and despised. Heaven, or paradise, might be defined as the place which men avoid.

I am tempted to put into the same category this startling sentence:

I should be pleased to meet man in the woods. I wish he were to be encountered like wild caribou and moose.

This is perhaps superficial cynicism. Deeper lie more searching meditations on man that to me, at least, are quite as good as anything in La Rochefoucauld. Here are four or five:

No innocence can quite stand up under suspicion, if it is conscious of being suspected. In the company of one who puts a wrong construction upon your actions, they are apt really to deserve a mean construction. While in that society I can never retrieve myself. Attribute to me a great motive, and I shall not fail to have one; but a mean one, and the fountain of virtue will be poisoned by the suspicion.

Again:

It is only by a sort of voluntary blindness, and omitting to see, that we know ourselves, as when we see stars with the side of the eye. . . . It is as hard to see one's self as to look backwards without turning round. And foolish are they that look in glasses with that intent.

Here is the kind of paradox the Frenchman liked to put:

What offends me most in my compositions is the moral element in them. The repentant say never a brave word. Their resolves should be mumbled in silence. Strictly speaking, morality is not healthy. Those undeserved joys which come uncalled and make us more pleased than grateful are they that sing.

Or again:

We cannot well do without our sins; they are the highway of our virtue.

This has the full flavor of the French seventeenth century.

Compliments and flattery oftenest excite my contempt by the pretensions they imply, for who is he that assumes to flatter me? To compliment often implies an assumption of superiority in the complimenter. It is, in fact, a subtle detraction.

140

Such a paragraph could be inserted without incongruity into the *Pensées* of Pascal.

The component of stoicism in Thoreau's outlook has been much discussed. Stoicism is an ambiguous word, but I have been struck by passage after passage in the *Journals* that expresses the temper of Marcus Aurelius in the *Meditations.* Here are representative instances:

It concerns us rather to be something here present than to leave something behind us.

Nature refuses to sympathize with our sorrow. She seems not to have provided for, but by a thousand contrivances against, it. She has bevelled the margins of the eyelids that the tears may not over-flow on the cheek.

If I have brought this weakness on my lungs, I will consider calmly and disinterestedly how the thing came about, that I may find out the truth and render justice. Then, after patience, I shall be a wiser man than before.

Of those noble deeds which have me for their object I am only the most fortunate spectator, and would rather be the abetter of their nobleness than stay their tide with the obstructions of im-patient gratitude.

Though the parents cannot determine whether the child shall be male or female, yet, methinks, it depends on them whether he shall be a worthy addition to the human family.

Possibly under this rubric should be put what is to me the saddest line in all Thoreau:

The bones of children soon turn to dust again.

The observation is, if you will, commonplace, but it comes from a childless man who hungered on his deathbed for the companionship of the young.

But the *sententiae* are not confined to the sad sincerity of the great Roman; they also have the warmth, humor, and vitality of Montaigne. Some of the passages on men of the ancient world might have been written by that essayist. For example:

The Greeks were boys in the sunshine, the Romans were men in the field, the Persians women in the house, the Egyptians old men in the dark.

The story of Romulus and Remus being suckled by a wolf is not mere fable; the founders of every state which has risen to eminence have drawn their nourishment and vigor from a similar source. It is because the children of the empire were not suckled by wolves that they were conquered and displaced by the children of the northern forests who were.

Thoreau's observations have also the genial quality of this master: "When I read the other day the weight of some of the generals of the Revolution, it seemed no unimportant fact in their biography. It is at least one other means of comparing ourselves with them." Surely, like Montaigne, Thoreau might have begun his journal with such a statement as: "C'est icy un livre de bon foy, lecteur," offering in proof such paragraphs as these:

Scholars have for the most part a diseased way of looking at the world. They mean by it a few cities and unfortunate assemblies of men and women, who might all be concealed in the grass of the prairies. They describe this world as old or new, healthy or diseased, according to the state of their libraries,—a little dust more or less on their shelves. When I go abroad from under this shingle or slate roof, I find several things which they have not considered.

And this:

Some faces that I see are so gross that they affect me like a part of the person improperly exposed, and it occurs to me that they might be covered, and, if necessary, some other, and perhaps better-looking, part of the person be exposed.

Or this:

Like cuttlefish we conceal ourselves, we darken the atmosphere in which we move; we are not transparent.

And finally I cite this remarkable piece of self-analysis:

I only know myself as a human entity, the scene, so to speak, of thoughts and affections, and am sensible of a certain doubleness by which I can stand as remote from myself as from another. However

142

intense my experience, I am conscious of the presence and criticism of a part of me, which, as it were, is not a part of me, but spectator, sharing no experience, but taking note of it, and that is no more I than it is you. When the play—it may be the tragedy of life—is over, the spectator goes his way. It was a kind of fiction, a work of the imagination only, so far as he was concerned.

These are but samplings of about 400 *sententiae* from the *Journals* alone. More could be found in the formal books. I have cited nothing from Thoreau's sardonic observations on New England church life, on politicians, on family relationships, on the structure and manners of society, on science, or on the races of men, though I think the following too interesting to omit: "There is always a slight haze or mist on the brow of an Indian. The white man's brow is clear and distinct. It is eleven o'clock in the forenoon with him. It is four o'clock in the morning with the Indian."

In categorizing many of the passages I have quoted as being like Voltaire or La Rochefoucauld, Marcus Aurelius or Montaigne, I wish neither to enter into a dreary debate over literary sources nor to derogate from the originality of Thoreau. I am merely trying to define him and to celebrate an aspect of his genius that seems to me neglected. Were we to extract from his writings the *sententiae* he wrote on human nature, human conduct, and human psychology, number them, and print them as separate paragraphs (as some of his observations on nature have been printed), we would have a book like the *Maximes* of La Rouchefoucauld, the *Pensées* of Pascal and the aphorisms of Lichtenberg. One does not have to be a student of transcendentalism to understand the force of an observation like: "Genius is inspired by its own works; it is hermaphroditic," nor to worry about Thoreau's college education to comprehend: "Do you suppose they were a race of consumptives and dyspeptics who invented Grecian mythology and poetry? The poet's words are, 'You would almost say the body thought.' I quite say it. I trust we have a good body then."

The moralist does not have to be tied to a system. It is enough that he gaze back and forth between his fellow beings and himself. Thoreau, I repeat, is in the French sense one of the great moralists of the Western world. We ought to restore this surveyor of Concord to his rightful place as a shrewd and candid observer of the motives and behavior of men. He observed humanity quite as objectively as he did the muskrat and the loon.

Poe, "The Raven," and the Anonymous Young Man

Previously published in *Western Humanities Review,* Vol. IX (Spring 1955), 127–138.

THE SHIFT in literary valuations that has exalted Melville, Hawthorne, and Henry James and lowered the esteem in which Bryant, Longfellow, Lowell, and others are held is probably irrevocable, whatever damage it does to literary history. We re-read the national classics to ascertain what they have to say to us, not what they have to say to the nineteenth century, and perhaps this is a kind of long-run justice. It is true that Bryant had a wide-ranging philosophic intelligence, that Longfellow is one of the great prosodists in American letters, and that Lowell was, until about 1910, ranked with Goethe and Arnold as a supreme example of the cultivated man of letters; but it is too late to reverse fashions in taste, even if one wanted to. The truly embarrassing figure in this transvaluation of values is not a New Englander of the Golden Day. It is Edgar Allan Poe.

He was once our great tragic figure, and we were re-enforced in this belief by the enthusiasm of Europe—for example, Baudelaire. He was our Berlioz, our Byron, our Fuseli. What is he now? He has been relegated to the source hunters and to the young: the source hunters are still turning up evidence of his liberal takings from other persons' work, and the young still shudder—at least I suppose they do—at "The Cask of Amontillado" and "The Masque of the Red Death." But Poe the man of mystery, Poe the idol of the romantics, Poe the creator of the philosophy of the short story, Poe the demon-haunted, Poe the solitary, Poe the supreme stylist, Poe of "Ulalume" and "The Raven"—Poe, it seems, was really none of these things, but a vulgarian, a journalist, a literary mechanic. If you want to realize his shallowness read "The Raven."

Typical of such contemporary judgment is Mr. W. H. Auden's critical introduction to selections from the prose and verse of Poe, published in the useful Rinehart editions. Mr. Auden obviously tries to be fair—he recalls, for example, the fine effect of "The Raven" and "The Bells" upon him in youth, and he remembers that "The Pit and the Pendulum" was one of the first short stories he read. Clearly, however, "Black Beauty" or "Hans Brinker," for neither of which one makes extravagant claims, is equally moving at that period of life. Mr. Auden, a modern, desires to correct our unfortunate juvenile tastes—in plain terms, if we must have Poe at all, he wants to substitute "The Narrative of Arthur Gordon Pym" and "Eureka" (taken together, they occupy over half his anthology) for that "inferior story," "The Cask of Amontillado," which he would omit, except that it would be "commercial suicide" to do so. I cannot, I confess, sustain the willing suspension of disbelief over the accumulated impossibilities of Pym's rather pointless career that I can for "The Cask of Amontillado." Mr. Auden wants to avoid complacency, yet—"Poor Poe!" he exclaims on the very first page, "today in danger of becoming the life study of a few professors!" Mr. Auden is not hopeful about professors. Poe's "major stories" have in common mainly a "negative characteristic," which is that "there is no place in any of them for the human individual," or if not that, then the central character cannot change but "only experience." I had thought that being condemned to "only experience" without the ability to change was one of the sources of Kafka's singular power, but apparently what is right for the author of *The Trial* is wrong for the author of "The Pit and the Pendulum."

146

Then there are the minor stories and sketches. The serious ones are, as one might expect, outmoded—"slightly vulgar and comic" is Mr. Auden's phrase, unless you indulgently remember that in the first half of the nineteenth century American taste was low, indeed. As for the comic ones, why, "Poe is not as funny in them as in some of his criticism." But in criticism, it seems, Poe "never developed to his full stature." This is probable enough, and much the same thing has been said of Coleridge. But Poe has had to sustain a special misfortune, or rather a double one: he was one of the earliest "to suffer *consciously* the impact of the destruction of the traditional community and its values," whatever that means; and he is "doomed to be used in school textbooks as a bait to interest the young in good literature, to be a respectable rival to the pulps." Somehow I find it difficult to conceive a man thrust out of the traditional community by the destruction of that community, serving as a bait for the young in that most communal of all institutions, the school system; but as it is fashionable nowadays to express literary self-pity in terms Poe seldom employed (this, I take it, is what is meant by "the destruction of the traditional community and its values"), let me turn to the test case of that vulgar poem, "The Raven."

But first let me say a word about Mr. Auden and the major stories. Of the horror stories and the tales of ratiocination Mr. Auden writes:

The problem in writing stories of this kind is to prevent the reader from ever being reminded of historical existence, for, if he once thinks of real people whose passions are interrupted by a need for lunch or whose beauty can be temporarily and mildly impaired by the common cold, the intensity and timelessness become immediately comic.

This is not all Mr. Auden has to tell us, and I do him injustice in isolating this passage from the totality of his remarks, but at any rate he makes this point. I think it is the wrong point to make, among other reasons because Mr. Auden's discussion of Poe's fiction turns upon a common contemporary idea —the "destructive passion of the lonely ego." I rather doubt that Poe had a "lonely ego" in mind when he wrote.

But let us turn to the problem of the luncheon and the common cold. There is considerable evidence that James's governess in "The Turn of the Screw" ate lunch regularly, but surely the point of that stupendous story does not concern either her nasal passages or her digestion but the enigma of evil in the world, just as the point of "Ligeia" is not the "destructive passion of the lonely ego" but the enigma of the human will, and the point of "The Fall of the House of Usher" is not Roderick's health, literally understood, but the general truth that thin partitions divide madness from sanity. Poe, who had a great deal of the eighteenth century in him, was far more interested in general propositions about mankind (witness the tales of ratiocination) than he was in the "destructive passion of the lonely ego." His style may be, as Mr. Auden rightly says, operatic, but the fundamental brainwork underlying his most emotional stories is rather more like that of Voltaire than it is like that of Mrs. Radcliffe. The thousand hardships Candide undergoes would kill a truly human individual, but most readers, untroubled by the common cold, are willing to accept the tacit premise that Candide is not a human individual but a puppet demonstrating a theorem. Poe's stories begin more like *contes* than they do like reality, even the "romantic" reality of, say, Balzac's "Passion in the Desert" or Mr. Robert Nathan's amusing *The Bishop's Wife.*

The *conte* does not pretend to be a slice of life, nor a mirror, nor any picture of a three-dimensional world in which imaginary people eat lunches and suffer the common cold. Rather, it is a sort of algebraic demonstration, in which the signs of operation are not X, Y, and Z, but symbols having human names (sometimes no names at all); and just as nobody actually buys X bushels of potatoes for Y money, and yet we arrive at useful truths by pretending there is a world of X, Y,

148

and Z, so it is with the *conte*. The *conte* never embraces the workaday premise of a week-end potato sale at the A & P. Nobody ever traveled so far or had so many remarkable thoughts in actual life as did Zadig in that story, just as nobody ever plotted murder with the cold skill and macabre cunning of Montresor in "The Cask of Amontillado," and nobody ever combined scientific curiosity and acute suffering as does the anonymous hero of "The Pit and the Pendulum." It seems to me Poe's peculiar success lies in his ability to begin with the *conte* and to end with the tale—that is, to begin with algebraic anonymity and then, just before the climax, to turn the situation, not into terms of the lonely ego, but into terms of generalized human significance.

Let me illustrate the point from three familiar stories. The first is this: Irritated by a thousand injuries culminating in insult, A decides to assassinate B, but in a manner at once consonant with B's amoral character and undiscoverable as against A. To do so, he must prepare and carry out his plans with the precision of a machine. This he does, but at the climatic moment his enemy appeals to God. A suddenly discovers that the mercy of God has removed B from the torture A had planned, and likewise that he (A) is not a thinking machine but a fallible human being; and though he entombs the body of his enemy and conceals his crime for half a century, he must at length confess by narrating it. This is, of course, "The Cask of Amontillado"; B is Fortunato and A is Montresor. Both are, up to the last page, mere symbols, like Candide or Pangloss. But when Fortunato cries out to God, Montresor is forced to confess his own human nature in the key sentence: "My heart grew sick; on account of the dampness of the catacombs," a statement that simultaneously endows him with weakness, pride, and hypocrisy. In short, the sense of tears in human things replaces algebra, and we are left, not with an equation, but with moral discourse.

Again: A man condemned to death passes into a state, half

coma, half hallucination, during which his senses are extraordinarily acute, and in that condition undergoes the subtlest of tortures, one which combines confinement of body with agony of soul. Just when his situation reaches the limits of the endurable, he hears a hum of voices, a blast of trumpets, and a harsh grating sound as the walls of his prison fly back. A friendly arm rescues him from falling into the pit. But the friendly arm has a nation back of it—the nation of humanity, for it is the arm of a French general who, entering Toledo, has overthrown the Inquisition. The tale ends in humane significance. (The Inquisition is, of course, part of the algebra of the story.)

A third example: A nameless man visits the remote home of a former companion, who lives with a sister. The friend is obviously on the verge of insanity. The sister seems to die, the friend buries her alive, she escapes from the tomb, confronts her brother, and kills him by virtue of the shock he experiences. "From that chamber, and from that mansion," says the anonymous "I," "I fled aghast." The house falls to ruin behind him. Looking back, we find the anonymous one has been throughout so wrapt in his own sensations and his own curiosity, he has done essentially nothing practical to aid his friend. It is not until the climax of the story that he is made to realize too late that sympathy is not enough, that he himself is partially responsible for the ruin he has chronicled. "Bending closely over him [Roderick Usher]," we read, "I *at length* drank in the hideous import of his words." Why *at length?* Because Poe wishes to humanize his ending, to bring his demonstration of the rationale of insanity into contact with the "outside" world. "The Fall of the House of Usher," though it is less like a *conte* than the other two, is nevertheless plotted as a demonstration that there are things in heaven and earth not dreamed of in our philosophy; but it ends, like a miracle of Our Lady, as a revelation of the true horror, which is spiritual sloth.

But let us get on to the poetry, concerning which Mr. Auden is forthright. Poe's best poems, he avers, are not the most typical or the most original of his verse. Mr. Auden omits "To Helen" ("Helen, thy beauty is to me"), which he thinks Landor could have written; but he prints "The City in the Sea," which he thinks Tom Hood might have written. To my ear, Hood could not possibly have achieved the prosodic dexterity of "The City in the Sea," for his dexterity, great as it is, always inclines to regularity; and as for "To Helen," the classical Landor would never have permitted himself the ambiguous syntax, the singular mixture of styles, nor the metrical irregularities of that haunting lyric.

But this is to be captious, and Mr. Auden interests himself in the general faultiness of Poe's verse. Of this faultiness the great example is "The Raven," concerning which Mr. Auden says that "the thematic interest and the prosodic interest, both of which are considerable, do not combine and are even often at odds." The artificiality of the lover asking a series of questions to which a single answer is ever to be returned is Poe's problem, and though in "The Philosophy of Composition" Poe tells us how he worked out the elements of his theme, his effect, says Mr. Auden, "could still be ruined unless the narration of the story, as distinct from the questions, flowed naturally." But Mr. Auden thinks it does not flow naturally because the meter, "with its frequent feminine rhymes, so rare in English, works against this." He quotes:

Not the least obeisance made he; not a minute stopped or stayed he;
But with mien of lord or lady, perched above my chamber door.

Here the meter "is responsible for the redundant alternatives of 'stopped or stayed he' and 'lord or lady.' "

Ever since the Imagist movement we have grown suspicious of mere redundancy in verse; and if we assume that the primary responsibility of the poem (or at least one of its primary responsibilities) is to give us a "natural flow" of language suitable to the speaker and the situation, Mr. Auden has a very strong point. Indeed, from this standpoint Mr. Auden is kinder to the poem than he should be. "The Raven," in the way of nature, has many more absurdities than "obeisance" and "lord or lady." Not merely the meter, but the whole setting is wrong. The window, simultaneously guarded by a lattice and a shutter; the physical impossibility of the raven sitting on a "pallid" bust (obviously, then, with the light in front of both bird and bust) and yet casting a shadow on the floor; the unfortunate cushioned seat with its incredible "velvet-violet lining"; the seraphim whose footfalls "tinkle on the tufted floor"; and, for that matter, a bird with a "shorn and shaven crest"—these things pile absurdity upon absurdity, without entering upon perplexing technical problems of trochaic meter, feminine rhyme, repetend, anacrusis, and so forth. Moreover, the lost Lenore is not particularized as her companion in sorrow, "The Blessed Damozel," is particularized. The damozel still has enough animal heat in her body to make the bar she leaned on warm, but Lenore is the mere shadow of a shade. The prosodic interest is certainly considerable—so considerable that, as in fascination we watch Poe's juggling, we may forget the thematic material altogether. Or perhaps the meter is simply wrong for the poem, as the meter of Wordsworth's poor Susan poem is wrong. In that poem it is difficult to experience simultaneously sympathetic nostalgia for the country, and the jig-time movement of: "There's a thrush that sings loud, it has sung for three years."

All this may or may not be true, but the difficulty is that when Mr. Auden, or I, or anybody else gets through demonstrating that Poe's poem simply will not do, "The Raven," never flitting, stays right where it was—a minor masterpiece, if you like, but masterpiece nevertheless. If one of the tests of a masterpiece is that it ends development along the particular line of its success, then "The Raven" succeeds. I saw, said Rossetti, that Poe had done all that could be done with the sorrowing lover on earth; and so in "The Blessed Damozel" Rossetti translated the whole idea into another sphere. It is curious that, precisely as there has been no second "Raven," so there has been no second "Damozel," however varied or amusing the library of parodies in either case. Moreover, the general observation applies not only to the substance but to the meter of Poe. Nobody has tried to use his stanza for serious purposes since his time— not even Swinburne, who took over the Rubáiyàt quatrain for "Laus Veneris," and whom no metrical difficulty could balk. If there is some mild debate about which way indebtedness flows between Poe and Thomas Holley Chivers, in the light of Poe's success, "Isadore" sounds even funnier than it would sound anyway:

> As an egg, when broken, never
> Can be mended, but must ever
> Be the same crushed egg forever—
> So shall this dark heart of mine!

Crushed eggs really brings us back to lunch and the world of the common cold.

Perhaps the meter and the theme are more harmonious than Mr. Auden realizes. But to demonstrate this, we ought first to discover what "The Raven" is all about.

Obviously it is a poem about an Anonymous Young Man. Now the Anonymous Young Man is a standard nineteenth-century hero. He suffers a great deal, especially in the first half of that immortal epoch, so much, indeed, that I cannot recall any literary work in which he is truly happy. He paces the shores of the sounding sea in "Locksley Hall," uttering a variety of morbid sentiments, and he goes mad in "Maud." His odd goings-on are chronicled by Bulwer-Lytton, Dickens, and Disraeli. He turns up in Matthew Arnold, he turns up in Clough's "Dipsychus," and he turns up as the thoughtful young man contemplating the harlot in Rossetti's "Jenny," as William C. De Vane has sympathetically demonstrated. He goes abroad, too, and writes the confession of a child of a century with the

153

pen of de Musset, and becomes a stoic with de Vigny. As an Italian he laments the brevity of life with Leopardi, as an American he is sensitive in Hawthorne, as a German he haunts that literature from Tieck through Heinrich Heine. Sometimes he has a name, but essentially he is anonymous. Elderly critics might refer to him as a stereotype, but contemporary refinement likes to call him a *persona*—a mask through which the writer speaks as a poet, not as a man.

Whether stereotype or *persona,* the Anonymous Young Man is a signal to the reader. He is not an ordinary, middle-class young man, well adjusted to society, comfortable in his religious beliefs, persuaded of the bourgeois virtues, and modeling himself upon Benjamin Franklin. The Anonymous Young Man is sensitive, morbid, and accursed. He likes to prowl around at night. He likes to experiment with drugs, hypnotism, music. Sometimes, as in the case of Bulwer's Pelham, he manages to throw off his doom by embracing a radical philosophy (in this case utilitarianism), but more commonly, like the modern Private Prewitt, his abnormality is so fixed, he embraces darkness like a bride. Unlike that unfortunate bugler, the Anonymous Young Man is much given to study, seeking in strange libraries some answer to the riddle of the painful earth. And always (again unlike Prewitt) he is confessional, not, I think, because of any "destructive passion of the lonely ego," but mostly because he just likes to talk. When, therefore, a reader in the 1840's picked up a new poem called "The Raven," he knew at once it was about the Anonymous Young Man:

Once upon a midnight dreary, while I pondered weak and weary,
Over many a quaint and curious volume of forgotten lore—

And as the detective story fan immediately asks himself, "What's the new gimmick in this one?" so the reader, when American taste was thus low in 1845, asked himself, "What is novel, what is strange about the Anonymous Young Man this time?" He read "The Raven" with certain expectations in mind. He expected the poet to establish a new variant in the psychology of the Anonymous Young Man.

Like almost everybody else who reads "The Philosophy of Composition," I am sceptical about it as an explanation of the origin of "The Raven." If we are to believe Poe, he achieved this poem by sheer ratiocination, which clearly he did not. But this does not mean that "The Raven" lacks the fundamental brainwork that goes into the making of a good poem; and if we put aside Poe's pompous discussion of "Beauty," and how the most beautiful of melancholy themes is the death of a beautiful woman, and how the true originality of his meter is not that it is octameter acatalectic, alternating with heptameter catalectic and terminating with tetrameter catalectic, but the stanza he has invented—if, I say, we put all this aside and look towards the end of his essay, we find something more valid. Here it is:

With the *dénouement* proper—with the Raven's reply, "Nevermore," to the lover's final demand if he shall meet his mistress in another world—the poem, in its obvious phase, that of a simple narrative, may be said to have its completion. So far, everything is within the limits of the accountable—of the real. A raven, having learned by rote the single word "Nevermore," and having escaped from the custody of its owner, is driven at midnight, through the violence of a storm, to seek admission at a window from which a light still gleams—the chamber-window of a student, occupied half in pouring over a volume, half in dreaming of a beloved mistress deceased. The casement being thrown open at the fluttering of the bird's wings, the bird itself perches on the most convenient seat out of the immediate reach of the student, who, amused by the incident and the oddity of the visitor's demeanor, demands of it, in jest and without looking for a reply, its name. The raven addressed, answers with its customary word, "Nevermore,"—a word which finds immediate echo in the melancholy heart of the student, who, giving utterance aloud to certain thoughts suggested by the occasion, is again startled by the fowl's repetition of "Nevermore." The student now guesses the state of the case, but is impelled . . . *by the human thirst for self-torture and in part by superstition,* to propound such queries to the bird as will bring him, the lover, the most of the luxury of sorrow, through the anticipated answer "Nevermore."

Two things are invariably required—first, some account of complexity, or more properly, adaptation; and, secondly, some amount of suggestiveness—*Some under-current, however indefinite, of meaning.* It is this latter, in especial, which imparts to a work of art so much of that *richness* . . . which we are too fond of confounding with the *ideal.* . . . I added the two concluding stanzas of the poem—their suggestiveness being thus made to pervade all the narrative which has preceded them. . . . It will be observed that the words, 'from out my heart,' involve the first metaphorical expression in the poem. They, with the answer, "Nevermore," dispose the mind to seek a moral in all that has been previously narrated. The reader begins now to regard the Raven as emblematical—but it is not until the very last line of the very last stanza that the intention of making him emblematical of *Mournful and Never-ending Remembrance is permitted distinctly to be seen.*

I have italicized two passages not italicized by Poe—that about self-torture and that about some undercurrent of meaning.

Premising the discussion by the fact that in Poe's day the word "moral" (as in Wordsworth's "all my moral being") was interchangeably used for "ethical" or "psychological" (sometimes it simultaneously meant both), we note Poe's insistence that the point of his poem is "to seek a moral" in what is narrated; i.e., to try to comprehend the ethico-psychic statement of "The Raven," or, more simply, to understand that here is an exercise in the psychology of the Anonymous Young Man. Three relatively abnormal motives, he says, have been introduced: the human thirst for self-torture; superstition; and "some under-current, however indefinite, of meaning." But "some under-current, however indefinite, of meaning" is a precise definition of surrealism; and in moving from the actual world to the "richness" implied by "the first metaphorical expression" in his production, Poe is, in a sense, reversing the movement of "The Fall of the House of Usher." In that story the hero escapes from a world in which haggard-eyed solitaries

156

play music more eerie than the so-called "Last Waltz of Von Weber" and bury their sisters alive, into the world of the accountable, of the real. But "The Raven," by contrary motion, moves out of an actual world in which, one stormy midnight, a trained raven finds shelter in a student's room, into a world in which seraphim swing censers, the demented hope for an answer from total darkness, a crazed young man asks unanswerable questions of a fowl, and, as a weird climax (suggestive of the "March to the Scaffold" in Berlioz's symphony), begs the bird to take its beak from out his (the student's) heart, albeit the bird is safely ensconced over the doorway. The bird is now transformed into as obscene a demonic symbol of utter cynicism as Faust anywhere meets on the Brocken, and is no longer an ordinary *corvus corax*. In plain terms, the Anonymous Young Man is now completely out of his head, displaying some of the classic attributes of schizophrenia, which, according to definition, is marked by "loss of contact with environment, and disintegration of personality." We are all too familiar with "The Raven"; but if we were not, we would catch the sheer, somnambulistic horror of its climax:

And the Raven, never flitting, still is sitting, *still* is sitting
On the pallid bust of Pallas just above my chamber door;
And his eyes have all the seeming of a demon's that is dreaming,
And the lamp-light o'er him streaming throws his shadow on the
    floor;
And my soul from out that shadow that lies floating on the floor
           Shall be lifted—never more!

Here, too, are "redundant alternatives"—"still is sitting," twice given; "shadow" likewise given twice; and here also the meter "with its frequent feminine rhymes, so rare in English," yields us "seeming," "streaming," "dreaming"—surely no brilliant discoveries by themselves. And here, likewise, are the heavy, the virtually mechanical, the excessive alliteration and assonance, which characterize the whole poem. But here also, after 108 lines which clearly do not "flow naturally," we

157

have our Anonymous Young Man turned into a monomaniac living in a surrealist universe—the bust and the raven, the queer light, the weird, theatrical shadow,[1] the hinted diablerie of the eyes of the dreaming bird, all very much like an invention of Salvador Dali. How does Poe manage this psychological transformation?

The process is that of hypnotizing both the Anonymous Young Man and the reader, and to this hypnosis the meter, together with the iteration of a few significant symbols inextricably caught up into the meter and coming relentlessly around with it, is the chief contributor. Obviously one such symbol is "tapping," which, with its synonym, appears eight times. Another such is "Lenore," which also appears eight times. A third, a little more difficult to define, is the element of light in the poem, in its struggle with darkness and death, which begins as dying embers creating their own ghosts and ends, after an invitation to the raven to return to "the Night's Plutonian shore," with the queer, unnatural lights of the last stanza— pallor on the bust, demonic eyes, streaming lamp-light, an impossible shadow, and the climactic ghastliness of "my soul from out that shadow that lies *floating* on the floor." Finally, there are various hints at the kind of levitation one experiences in nightmares—the curtains that strangely rustle of themselves, the grotesque unwilled movement of the bird from the window to the door, the odd sensations of "wheeled a cushioned seat," "upon the velvet sinking," "divining, with my head at ease reclining," the movement of the seraphim, the eventual uprush of the figure in the chair, and, of course, the floating of the shadow at the ominous end.

Essential to the hypnotic effect is repetition—the going over and over again of the same words, the same ideas, the same images in the same order. Mr. Auden's complaint about the

[1] Poe's explanation that he had in mind a "bracket candelabrum . . . high above the door and bust" reads to me like an explanation after the fact.

158

"redundant alternatives" he cites gets at the matter, it seems to me, in the wrong way. The slow drag of the narrative, the pondering such trivia as the distinction between "stopped" and "stayed," "rapping" and "tapping," "rare and radiant," "faintly" and "gently," "soon again," "flirt and flutter"—do these not simultaneously slow up the movement of events and create the queer, hypochondriacal kind of wrong-headed particularity characteristic of a mind in this situation? The nineteenth century, at least, thought so—witness Dr. Manette's recurrence to tapping on shoe leather in *The Tale of Two Cities.* The rhythmic repetition of a set of *idées fixes,* with sufficient variation cunningly to call attention to the monotony—is not this no small part of Poe's success in the poem?

In "The Raven" time stands still. We have but one indication of temporality—"a midnight dreary"—but all the actions of the Anonymous Young Man occur in a region beyond time. The sense of escaping temporal limitations begins with the frustration of the second stanza, where tomorrow never comes; passes into the fantastic heartbeats of the following unit, curiously echoed in the meter; transforms itself into the endless moment of staring into darkness; and then, so to speak, disappears with the entrance of the Raven, the fantastic dialogue, and the final frozen instant when the Anonymous Young Man, instead of banishing the bird as he had hoped, finds it (like the albatross) translated out of ornithology into eternity. But this mounting crescendo towards an endless and horrible Now is possible only because of the metrical structure of the whole.

Some of the lines are, indeed, ridiculous (for example: "For we cannot help agreeing that no living human being"), and some of the images vulgar ("whose velvet-violet lining with the lamp-light gloating o'er"). One feels that the chamber, which Poe evidently got up in high romantic style, is mostly Biedermeier Gothic. But the important thing is not the bad coloring, the lapses in taste, or the high-flown language in which the Anonymous Young Man carries on his dialogue with the Raven; the important thing is that "The Raven" overrides bad taste and absurdity largely by reason of its superb metrical structure—the monotony-in-variety that Poe managed to give his theme. Thus 54 lines rhyme with "nevermore"; of these, 37 are on precisely five syllables (door [adore], floor, Lenore, before, and the "plore" of implore and explore), but few readers not interested in metrical technique notice this, so cunningly is the metrical movement arranged to carry the terminal rhymes.

It would be curious to inquire into other elements of Poe's success—for example, the concealed but growing hyperaesthesia of the Anonymous Young Man, who begins with normal hearing and then harkens to seraphic footfalls, and who passes from a half somnolent state (if, indeed, the whole poem is not a nightmare) into the self-torture, as Poe calls it, of hysterical questionings. The meter holds together superbly the two elements that compel a willing suspension of disbelief until the poem is done—namely, the grotesque and the maniacal; and I do not see, once one has mastered the true theme of the piece, that the prosodic interest and the thematic interest are anywhere antithetic, but rather that they are one and indissoluble. I am sure Poe sincerely believed that in "The Raven" he was celebrating that most melancholy of themes, the death of a beautiful woman, but the saintly Lenore is never described, and all that we know about her is that she is with the angels. What is presented, and powerfully presented, is, however, the movement from sanity to monomania in the "soul" of the Anonymous Young Man of the period; and this is managed by prosodic devices so powerful that nobody has since dared to imitate them.

Whittier Reconsidered

Prepared for the Whittier centennial and previously printed in *Essex Institute Historical Collections,* Vol. XCIII (October 1957), 231–246.

N<small>O POET</small> more cogently illustrates than Whittier does the transvaluation of values that has quietly taken place in American literary history during the last half century. When he died in 1892, there was small doubt that his was a major voice. Today it is a real question whether he is read at all except by children and students. The one-hundred-and-fiftieth anniversary of his birth finds no critic interested in him as critics are interested in Whitman, his fellow in the Quaker tradition. No literary historian is concerned to "place" Whittier in our intellectual development; and the scholars are few who work at the text of his writings, the exhumation of uncollected verse and prose, or the enrichment of his biography. The magnificent bibliography by Thomas F. Currier cannot be bettered as a piece of workmanship; it is not Mr. Currier's fault that it has the air of a mausoleum. The *Literary History of the United States* remarks with justice that *The Life and Letters of John Greenleaf Whittier* by Samuel T. Pickard, revised just fifty years ago, is still the best biography.[1]

It was not always so. The "Yard of American Poets" that

---

[1] Both Whitman Bennett's *Whittier: Bard of Freedom* (Chapel Hill, 1944) and John A. Pollard's *John Greenleaf Whittier: Friend of Man* (Boston, 1949) tend to concentrate upon the social reformer, not the poet as artist.

used to hang in many a schoolroom included Whittier along with Lowell, Longfellow, Bryant, and Holmes. The game of Authors played by Edwardian children allotted four cards to Whittier; and my recollection is that the cards were named "Barbara Frietchie," "Snow-Bound," "Maud Muller"—and what was the fourth? The fatal capacity of the mind, noted by Holmes, when it has to remember n things, to remember n-1 things intervenes. Was it "Ichabod"? "The Lost Occasion"? "The Eternal Goodness"? I do not know; but the fourth item, like the other three, implied moral improvement, I am sure, in terms simpler and more direct than those in Mr. Faulkner's celebrated Nobel Prize address.

> Our fathers to their graves have gone;
> Their strife is past, their triumph won;
> But sterner trials wait the race
> Which rises in their honored place;
> A moral warfare with the crime
> And folly of an evil time.

So Whittier. Mr. Faulkner carries on his own peculiar kind of moral warfare, I do not doubt, but it is not that of "Skipper Ireson's Ride," a poem that is now about a hundred years old. The modern reader needs to be told that Skipper Ireson, for his hard heart, was tarred, feathered, and carried in a cart by the women of Marblehead. One also remembers (or at least the scholar does) Whittier's handsome apology prefixed to his later printings of the poem after he had learned that his historical sources did not substantiate the story, just as one remembers the fine charity of the headnote prefixed in 1888 to "Ichabod." I wonder if any modern author is capable of this moral courtesy?

Something, it is clear, has vanished from our literary life. Christian gentlemanliness is out of key with the world of literary agents, book promotion, publishers' scouts, cocktail parties, and astringent academic quarterlies. What has vanished may be the genteel tradition. Or it may be politeness, or self-effacement, or idealism, or what you will. Anyway, it is gone, and the national life is presumably the poorer in its passing.

However one may lament the loss, lamentation does not, alas! improve either the art or the intellectual stature of this diffuse poet, now perpetually assigned to the schoolroom and the harmless introductory course in American literature. Especially have we turned our backs upon the public rhetoric of Whittier's verse; and though the Civil War annually produces its library of new books, our interest in that titantic conflict fails to revive the indignation Whittier poured into his rhymed attacks on slaveholders. Possibly the abolitionists have been so deflated by modern historians, his wrath seems hollow today, his indignation misplaced. Certainly he knew nothing of slavery from experience.

When we inquire into this problem, we are led to a neglected area of literary theorizing—the durability of indignation. It is easy to say that once a cause is won, the need for anger vanishes. Seventeenth-century pamphlets in which Christian sectaries called down fire from heaven upon those who disagreed with them are now of antiquarian interest only. Even to the historian their interest lies not in the indignation but in the context and the causes of the quarrel. It takes a learned footnote to apprise us that Dante consigned Venedigo Caccianimico to hell for local reasons. We do not care. Thomas Moore pouring his pint pot of vitriol over Thomas Jefferson in a bad poem does not infect us with the poet's contempt for Jefferson; he merely creates in us a passing contempt for Moore. In the same way we read with wonder the vocabulary of abuse showered on Ibsen when *Ghosts* began its painful conquest of the European stage, not because the vocabulary is startling, but because it is stale.

But the problem has another dimension—that of monotony. It is rhetorically easier to denounce a man than it is to define him. Since the vituperative writer wants to enlist a large public on his side, he employs words that quickly appeal. He confines his style to a minimal repetitious vocabulary. He reiterates that So-and-so is a red or a traitor, in obedience to the law that if you throw enough mud, some of it will stick, because defence must always be slow, patient, and particularistic. There is nothing subtle in angry writing.

Now and then, to be sure, a memorable phrase, a magnificent passage, a special and terrible anger promotes denunciation into mastership. The Old Testament, Juvenal, and the Divine Comedy have their moments of indignant greatness, and so has Voltaire, so has Victor Hugo or Swinburne. The spectacle of the little bard of Putney hurling his thunderbolts at Pio Nono and Napoleon III has its ludicrous aspects, but there is stylistic felicity in some of the *Dirae* sonnets that makes us forget the occasion and admire the white-hot fire. Individual phrases likewise occasionally calcine into perfection; as, for example, John Randolph's memorable description of the supposed alliance between Henry Clay and John Quincy Adams as a combination of the puritan and the blackleg, a coalition of Blifil and Black George. This is finely said. Waiving all questions of the justice of the thing, I recall from the days when William Hale Thompson, then major of Chicago, was threatening King George upon his throne, a letter in the Chicago *Tribune* that has always seemed to me classical: "Sir: The mention of the name of William Hale Thompson in any connection with the presidency of the United States is obscene. Yours very truly." I have forgotten the signature, but the letter is masterly.

In his anti-slavery poems Whittier rarely achieved marmoreal perfection. He reached it in "Ichabod"—

> . . . from those great eyes
> The soul has fled:
> When faith is lost, when honor dies,
> The man is dead!

But most of the anti-slavery pieces shriek and yell. Here, for instance, are some lines from a poem of 1832 addressed to Garrison:

> Long as one human heart shall swell
> Beneath the tyrant's rod.
>
> .   .   .   .
>
> To shake aloft his vengeful brand,
> And rend his chain apart.
>
> .   .   .   .
>
> Go on, the dagger's point may glare
> Amid thy pathway's gloom.

I know little about dagger points, but I doubt that they glare. Take "Expostulation" (1834), the opening stanza of which rhymes "law" with "war" and then compounds the offence by writing in "Eu*taw*" only four words later. Next, forced by the rhyme, it thrusts Sergeant Jasper of Fort Moultrie fame into the impossible task of rescuing the patriots' banner from a well.

> Our fellow-country men in chains!
>   Slaves, in a land of light and law!
> Slaves, crouching on the very plains
>   Where rolled the storm of Freedom's war!
> A groan from Eutaw's haunted wood,
>   A wail where Camden's martyrs fell,
> By every shrine of patriot blood,
>   From Moultrie's wall and Jasper's well!

This is writing for the mob. In "Laus Deo," a poem of jubilation at the adoption of the thirteenth amendment, when Whittier wanted to express genuine rapture, he had so exhausted his primitive vocabulary, he fell back upon the 28th chapter of Job and the 15th chapter of Exodus for figure and speech. Even in a relatively successful piece like "The Farewell of a Virginia slave mother to her daughters, sold in Southern bondage," the street speaker gets in the way of the poem:

> There no mother's eye is near them,
> There no mother's ear can hear them;
> Never when the torturing lash
> Seams their back (*sic!*) with many a gash,
> Shall a mother's kindness bless them,
> Or a mother's arms caress them.

This is in the best manner of Bulwer-Lytton's *Richelieu*.

The critic must, I fear, go farther. The twenty-odd volumes of verse that Whittier published indicate his fatal inability to distinguish between having a poem to write and having to write a poem. The occasional verse, to which he was professionally addicted, is for the most part, rhetoric. "The Shoemakers," for example, appears in all the college anthologies, but it is mere meter, not a meter-making argument. A poem addressed in 1851 to Kossuth, to take another example, is in the line of the anti-slavery pronouncements, sounding

> . . . the hoarse note of the bloodhound's baying,
> The wolf's long howl behind the bondman's flight.

Even the rhymed address to Burns, occasioned by "receiving a sprig of heather in blossom," though full of honorable sentiments, is diffuse (it runs to 116 lines) as Burns is seldom diffuse and concludes with ten moralizing stanzas on the frailties of the author of "The Cotter's Saturday Night."

When we ask why this sort of thing interests Whittier, we confront a principal but unacknowledged difference between the uses of poetry in the nineteenth century and its uses in the twentieth. In the nineteenth century, particularly during its first fifty years, the poet fulfilled a function he has since abandoned. He wrote for the newspapers, and in writing for the newspapers he was at once, or at times, columnist, editorial writer, cartoonist, and propaganda maker. Thus it was that Coleridge rhymed for the Tory papers and Moore wrote for the Whig journals. Thus it was that Tom Hood sparkled. Moreover, the century was the period of the album and the giftbook. Explorers of the bibliographies of even highly

166

respectable nineteenth-century bards must be puzzled by the many items first published in these ephemeral volumes or in the newspapers, but this form of publication explains in some degree the popularity of the writer. Newspaper verses were clipped by readers or republished by other members of the free and independent press, and contributions to the giftbooks turned up afterwards in all sorts of unexpected places. A specious currency was given to many names (for example, that of Felicia Hemans), including names of a more perdurable sort, and one suspects that many a poet was led to confuse poetry and journalism. One can hardly imagine a T. S. Eliot or a Wallace Stevens mistaking the art of the newspapers for the art of poetry.

Is Whittier no more than a producer of rhymed rhetoric that, however effective in its time, has lost its fire and energy? Is there no portion of his work that can still give aesthetic pleasure? If we will but remember Pater's injunction that beauty has been produced in many periods in many styles and in many forms, I think one can find even today a small but permanent portion of beauty in Whittier. That portion is not, I think, in popular and facile successes like "Maud Muller" and "Barbara Frietchie," but is rather found in three sorts of poems: those in which he writes about nature in New England; those in which (alas, too rarely!) he presents character; and those which concern—how shall I put it?—his notion of the relation of God and man.

One must distinguish between sentimentality and simplicity. Whittier, however manly in his private life, is incorrigibly given to sentimentality—far more so than is Longfellow. But there is in him likewise a vein of honest simplicity, particularly when he looks at the natural world about him, that anticipates and parallels the later effects of Robert Frost. I doubt that "The Last Walk in Autumn" is widely known, and I shall therefore quote rather more of its opening stanzas than I should otherwise do:

I

O'er the bare woods, whose outstretched hands
　　Plead with the leaden heavens in vain,
I see, beyond the valley lands,
　　The sea's long level dim with rain.
Around me all things, stark and dumb,
　　Seem praying for the snows to come,
And, for the summer bloom and greeness gone,
With winter's sunset lights and dazzling morn atone.

II

Along the river's summer walk,
　　The withered tufts of asters nod;
And trembles on its arid stalk
　　The hoar plume of the golden-rod.
And on a ground of sombre fir,
　　And azure-studded juniper,
The silver birch its buds of purple shows,
And scarlet berries tell where bloomed the sweet wild-rose!

III

With mingled sound of horns and bells,
　　A far-heard clang, the wild geese fly,
Storm-sent, from Arctic moors and fells,
　　Like a great arrow through the sky,
Two dusky lines converged in one,
　　Chasing the southward-flying sun;
While the brave snow-bird and the hardy jay
Call to them from the pines, as if to bid them stay.

IV

I passed this way a year ago;
　　The wind blew south; the noon of day
Was warm as June's; and save that snow
　　Flecked the low mountains far away,
And that the vernal-seeming breeze
　　Mocked faded grass and leafless trees,
I might have dreamed of summer as I lay,
Watching the fallen leaves with the soft wind at play.

V

Since then, the winter blasts have piled
　　The white pagodas of the snow
On these rough slopes, and, strong and wild,
　　Yon river, in its overflow

Of springtime rain and sun, set free,
    Crashed with its ices to the sea;
And over these gray fields, then green and gold,
The summer corn has waved, the thunder's organ rolled.

VI

Rich gift of God! A year of time!
    What pomp of rise and shut of day,
What hues wherewith our Northern clime
    Makes autumn's dropping woodlands gay,
What airs outblown from ferny dells,
    And clover-bloom and sweetbrier smells,
What songs of brooks and birds, what fruits and flowers,
Green woods and moonlit snows, have in its round been ours!

.   .   .   .

XXV

Then let the icy north-wind blow
    The trumpets of the coming storm,
To arrowy sleet and blinding snow
    Yon slanting lines of rain transform.
Young hearts shall hail the drifted cold,
    As gaily as I did of old;
And I, who watch them through the frosty pane,
Unenvious, live in them my boyhood o'er again.

This is, to be sure, thoroughly nineteenth-century stuff; and most of the poem, though pleasantly autobiographical, concerns moral, religious and psychological problems that have but a tangential relation to the natural setting of the whole poem. Some of the lines, it must be admitted, have a late eighteenth-century rhetorical flavor, suggestive of the heirs of Thomson's *Seasons,* as, for example, "The trumpets of the coming storm" and "The summer corn has waved, the thunder's organ rolled," whereas "Rich gift of God! A year of time!" calls up Young's *Night Thoughts,* that stately rhetorical mausoleum. Nor are "vernal-seeming breeze," "dropping woodlands gay" and "drifted cold" much better. Yet, when all is said, Whittier is not only entitled to applause for acute observation, as in "The hoar plume of the golden-rod," as Tennyson might be, but the whole passage is genuine, a transcript

169

of experience. We not only applaud, we instinctively acquiesce in "The sea's long level dim with rain," and in the picture of the wild geese—"Two dusky lines converged in one"—chasing the southerning sun. We even accept

> . . . airs outblown from ferny dells,
> And clover-bloom and sweetbrier smells

because we feel that the poet has crushed the sweetfern in his walks, and inhaled the odors of clover and sweetbrier. It is, to be sure, descriptive poetry; it is not poetry in which the psychology of the writer interpenetrates the universe and writes a gigantic ego across the sky, but it is, somehow, "true," and we accept it with pleasure because it shows how good and simple and direct the nineteenth century at its best could be in verses of this sort. There is more of this excellence in Whittier than readers are aware of. Alas, that it seldom concentrates in a single poem! Yet there are lovely passages scattered through the "Narrative and Legendary Poems," the "Poems of Nature," and the "Personal Poems" of the collected edition—as, "The Garrison of Cape Ann," the prelude to "Among the Hills," "Hampton Beach," "The River Path," and "In Peace," with its quiet opening:

> A track of moonlight on a quiet lake,
> Whose small waves on a silver-sanded shore
> Whisper of peace.

Our contemporary poets cannot give us this calm acceptance of Nature as a beautiful entity unmixed with human passion.

I have remarked upon the virtues of some, at least, of Whittier's presentations of character. I do not mean the featureless Maud Muller or the equally featureless Barbara Frietchie, nor, it must be confessed, can I refer without embarrassment to most of the narrative verse, of which Whittier composed a great deal. These share his commonest weakness—diffusion. But ever and again an anecdote, a character gripped him, and he curbed his tendency to wander and really sketched a memorable personality. Oddly enough, these are often rabbinical legends, "Rabbi Ishmael" being a case in point. But I think

I should choose as preëminent in this kind of writing the admirable "Abraham Davenport," which in a mere sixty-five lines gives us a picture, presents a character, and sums up a culture. Again, because it is not commonly known, the poem is worth quoting *in extenso:*

In the old days (a custom laid aside
With the breeches and cocked hats) the people sent
Their wisest men to make the public laws.
And so, from a brown homestead, where the Sound
Drinks the small tribute of the Mianas,
Waved over by the woods of Rippowams,
And hallowed by pure lives and tranquil deaths,
Stamford sent up to the councils of the State
Wisdom and grace in Abraham Davenport.

'Twas on a May-day of the far old year
Seventeen hundred eighty, that there fell
Over the blooms and sweet life of the Spring,
Over the fresh earth and the heaven of noon,
A horror of great darkness, like the night
In day of which the Norland sagas tell,—
The Twilight of the Gods. The low-hung sky
Was black with ominous clouds, save where its rim
Was fringed with a dull glow, like that which climbs
The crater's side from the red hell below.
Birds ceased to sing, and all the barn-yard fowls
Roosted; the cattle at the pasture bars
Lowed, and looked homeward; bats on leathern wings
Flitted abroad; the sounds of labor died;
Men prayed and women wept; all ears grew sharp
To hear the doom-blast of the trumpet shatter
The black sky, that the dreadful face of Christ
Might look from the rent clouds, not as he looked
A loving guest at Bethany, but stern
As Justice and inexorable Law.

Meanwhile in the old State House, dim as ghosts,
Sat the lawgivers of Connecticut,
Trembling beneath their legislative robes.
"It is the Lord's Great Day! Let us adjourn,"
Some said; and then, as if with one accord,
All eyes were turned to Abraham Davenport.
He rose, slow cleaving with his steady voice

The intolerable hush. "This well may be
The Day of Judgment which the world awaits;
But be it so or not, I only know
My present duty, and my Lord's command
To occupy till He come. So at the post
Where He hath set me in His providence,
I choose, for one, to meet Him face to face,—
No faithless servant frightened from my task,
But ready when the Lord of the harvest calls;
And therefore, with all reverence, I would say,
Let God do His work, we will see to ours.
Bring in the candles." And they brought them in.

Then by the flaring lights the Speaker read,
Albeit with husky voice and shaking hands,
An act to amend an act to regulate
The shad and alewive fisheries. Whereupon
Wisely and well spake Abraham Davenport,
Straight to the question, with no figures of speech
Save the ten Arab signs, yet not without
The shrewd dry humor natural to the man:
His awe-struck colleagues listening all the while,
Between the pauses of his argument,
To hear the thunder of the wrath of God
Break from the hollow trumpet of the cloud.

And there he stands in memory to this day,
Erect, self-poised, a rugged face, half seen
Against the background of unnatural dark,
A witness to the ages as they pass,
That simple duty hath no place for fear.

I do not know whether E. A. Robinson read this, but it anticipates the goodness of "Isaac and Archibald" and surpasses
that admirable piece in being concentrated.

The secret of the excellence of "Abraham Davenport" lies in
its fusion of low relief with salient observations. The metrical
tone is faint, like Crabbe's, but the pattern is always *there,*
is always gently persistent so that it can carry even the formal
description of the threatening sky without melodrama. Against
its gentle beat various important observations seem projected
by an impulse that is partly respect, partly humor. We laugh
at what we love, and obviously, Whittier loves Abraham

Davenport and can therefore afford to laugh at him a little. Note the amusing repetition of verbs placed first in the line, towards the end of the second section—"roosted," "lowed," "flitted," and then the variation that follows—"men prayed and women wept." The deliberate simplicity of " 'Bring in the candles.' And they brought them in," cannot be bettered in its place, nor can the contrast between the husky voice and shaking hands of the Speaker and the mock solemnity of

> An act to amend an act to regulate
> The shad and alewise fisheries.

The writer is so at ease with his material, he can take time out for a little play with figures of speech and figures of arithmetic; and even the last line, which in another poem—say, "Conductor Bradley"—might be tedious, is caught up in the wonderful atmosphere of irony and heroism, admiration and anticlimax Whittier achieves. Indeed, the irony of the penultimate "A witness to the ages as they pass" might be that of Frost or Robinson.

Whittier's ballads seldom come off, but *Snow-Bound: A Winter Idyl* remains a delight to those capable of reading it. I say "capable of reading it" for the reason that Whittier, like Mendelssohn, cannot be approached as if he were Bartok or Ives. The poem overcomes its flaws. The little sketches of personalities and the reflections they occasion are admirable in their kind. And, somehow, the final address to the "Angel of the backward look," despite its obviousness, does not offend; it fits the mood of the poem, placing "these Flemish pictures of old days" in right perspective. The work *is* an idyl (we commonly overlook the subtitle) and is therefore entitled to its mood of idyllic nostalgia for something lovely and lost. The opening is properly famous; and the line-by-line heaping up of detail about the storm and about the effect of the storm upon human life has the ring of truth and simplicity. "I read the other day," writes Emerson at the opening of "Self-Reliance," "some verses written by an eminent painter which were original and not conventional. The soul always hears an admonition in such lines, let the subject be what it may." The soul hears an admonition in *Snow-Bound:* an admonition not too hastily to throw away the past. In the poem the beauty of memory is made the more poignant because of the "restless sands' incessant fall," the importunate hours that bid "The dreamer leave his dream midway." We know the life of *Snow-Bound* as we know the village of Grand-Pré in *Evangeline,* the House of Seven Gables, the Old Manse, and Thoreau's cabin at Walden Pond. They are part of our inheritance, which no incessantness of teaching can wholly obliterate.

Religious verse of the first water by American writers is small in quantity, but this small anthology of Christian utterance Whittier contributes. The instinct that breaks "The Eternal Goodness" into smaller units and uses these for singing in our Protestant churches is, I think, sound. To be sure, God is also a mighty fortress, but there are many mansions in heaven with room for gentleness and peace. In such poems Whittier is at his best unsurpassed. What writer in English can better the serenity of stanzas like these?

> And so beside the Silent Sea
> I wait the muffled oar;
> No harm from Him can come to me
> On ocean or on shore.
>
> I know not where His islands lift
> Their fronded palms in air;
> I only know I cannot drift
> Beyond His love and care.

Whittier has, I suppose, only so much of mysticism as the Quaker faith allows. His poetry expresses no dark night of the soul; yet, believing that "God should be most where man is least," he has his flashes of marvelous quietude: "Where pity dwells, the peace of God is there," he writes in one poem, and in another:

> Here let me pause, my quest forego;
> Enough for me to feel and know
> That He in whom the cause and end,
> The past and future, meet and blend,—

174

> Who, girt with his Immensities,
> One vast and star-hung system sees,
> Small as the clustered Pleiades,—
> Moves not alone the heavenly quires,
> But waves the spring-time's grassy spires,
> Guards not archangel feet alone,
> But deigns to guide and keep my own.

There are too many *s*-sounds in the antepenultimate line in this passage, but this, one of the best portions of "Questions of Life," seems to me finely fashioned. Here again, however, diffuseness is the fatal flaw. "Andrew Rykman's Prayer," which has all the potentialities of a notable religious expression, goes on and on. The present state of literary criticism is indifferent or hostile to religious poetry unless it take the form of high church Anglicanism; and so we forget that no American writer has more finely phrased a trust in the goodness of God.

In Whittier this trust is not only part of the religious tradition into which he was born; it is counterpart to the one over-riding consideration in all his verse, which is Time itself. No American writer is more conscious of transience:

> So when Time's veil shall fall asunder,
> The soul may know
> No fearful change, nor sudden wonder,
> Nor sink the weight of mystery under,
> But with the upward rise, and with the vastness grow,

he writes in "Hampton Beach," all in the best manner of Victorian optimism, but nevertheless Time is incessant, Time takes away the loveliest and the best, Time closes the schoolhouse by the road, and Time occasions the much quoted "moral" of "Maud Muller." There is here no originality of thought or of interpretation, but Whittier again and again avails himself of what I may call the temporal fallacy to achieve his poetical effects. Thus *Snow-Bound* is seen, as it were, down a long tunnel of Time, its colors the clearer, its outlines the sharper by reason of the fact that the poet is almost sixty; and Whittier most applauds those who can look through the veil of Time and know it for illusion. Autumn attracts him as it does Archibald MacLeish because it is the human season; and in the Cambridge edition of the *Complete Poetical Works* I find it of some significance that "My Triumph" succeeds *Snow-Bound,* and opens:

> The autumn-time has come;
> On woods that dream of bloom
> And over purpling vines,
> The low sun fainter shines.
> The aster-flower is failing,
> The hazel's gold is paling;
> Yet overhead more near
> The eternal stars appear!

Contrasts of time and eternity are the commonplaces of poetry; my point is only that in so far as he is mystic, Whittier, troubled by the "harder task of standing still," as he somewhere says, meets the implications of time more immediately as a part of his problem of faith and progress than careless readers perceive. You can see him at his obvious worst on this theme in a poem like "The New Year," but you can also find his unexpected excellence in a poem like "The Prayer of Agassiz":

> Him, the endless, unbegun,
> The Unnamable, the One
> Light of all our Light the Source,
> Life of life, and Force of force

But one returns, as one must always return in this category of his art, to the marvel of stanzas like these from "Our Master":

> But warm, sweet, tender, even yet
> A present help is He;
> And faith has still its Olivet,
> And love its Galilee.
> The healing of His seamless dress
> Is by our beds of pain;
> We touch Him in life's throng and press,
> And we are whole again.

Not even the seventeenth century can surpass the simple perfection of this religious statement.

176

HISTORY AND THE CONTEMPORARY